BOOMERANGS AND CRACKAJACKS

THE HARMONICA IN AUSTRALIA
1825 to 1960

RAY GRIEVE

First published in 2014 by Ray Grieve
Bushlarkmusic www.bushlarkmusic.com
ISBN: 978-1925023848
Revised Edition published in 2019
ISBN:
Launched at the 2014 National Folk Festival
Canberra ACT Australia
by Kevin Bradley
Director of Sound Preservation and Senior Curator Research Collection
National Library of Australia

This book is copyright. Apart from any fair
dealing for the purpose of private study, research
or review, as permitted under the copyright Act,
no part may be reproduced by any process without
written permission. Inquiries concerning publication,
translation or recording rights should be addressed to the
author or publishers.

NATIONAL LIBRARY OF AUSTRALIA CIP DATA

Grieve, Ray.
Boomerangs and Crackajacks
(The Harmonica in Australia 1825 to 1960)

Includes Index.

1. Harmonica music. 2. Harmonica players - Australia
1. Title

WARNING: Indigenous Australians and Torres
Strait Islanders are warned that this book may contain
photographic images of deceased persons.

About the Author

Ray Grieve was a vocalist and rhythm guitarist in 1960's Sydney rock and blues bands including the Elliot Gordon Union. He played flute and tin whistle in traditional Australian folk bands and was one of the founding members of The Rouseabouts, within The Bush Music Club in the 1970s.

In the 1980s he began the research and collection of material on the history of the harmonica in Australia. The result of this research was his book "A Band in a Waistcoat Pocket" published by Currency Press and the companion tape and CD sets of original historic Australian mouth organ recordings released by Larrikin Records and launched by Larry Adler in 1995.

He has released two independent CD albums by his band Bushlark, performing vocals, flute, tin whistles and other various folk-wind instruments titled: "Reedy River Flute" (2000) and "For Now" (2007).

Twenty Bushlark band videos and audio tracks are available on YouTube and CD Baby outlets

Contents

Acknowledgements
Introduction

A Very Early Arrival   1
   In 1825, the first shipments of mouth organs arrived in the fledging Colony.
   They would eventually enjoy fame on the stage and public admiration
   in the Australian International Exhibitions.

Australian by Name   17
   In the late 1890s, the mouth organ acquired an Australian brand name
   and was included in the Commonwealth Celebrations of 1901 as well as in
   poems and limericks.

Off to War and into School   31
   By 1915, the mouth organ was the favourite instrument of Australian
   children and went on to gain further popularity with the soldiers of
   World War I.

Champions, Kings and Professors   39
   National Championships and the introduction of the wireless brought
   fame to many Australian players.

The Dark Side of the Mouth Organ   55
   As 'the instrument of the people', the harmonica was at times involved
   in the seamier side of life and played a part in some tragic events.

The Chromatic Harmonica and Another War   67
   World War II resulted in the break-up of Australia's mouth organ bands,
   but the period also saw the introduction of a technically superior form of
   the instrument.

The Professionals   79
   After the War, the chromatic harmonica was seen as a more 'legitimate'
   instrument than the diatonic with a new group of professional players
   emerging on the stage and television.

Mouth Organ Memorabilia   95
   Retailers' paraphernalia, tutors, recordings and rare examples of the
   instrument itself, are highly sought after by collectors, world-wide.

Harmonica Legends Reunited   103
   The story behind the book "A Band in Waistcoat Pocket" and a look at
   how it reunited Australia's harmonica legends.

Acknowledgements

Thank you to the following archives and libraries for permission to reproduce photographs:
Courtesy of the Australian War Memorial (p.77), OT 4964
City of Sydney Archives (p.39), NSCA CRS 51/304
Melbourne Library Service (p.42)
National Library of Australia (pp.5, 39, 90), NLA PIC an 8329195, vn3639168, an 24377422, an 24377447
NLA Newspapers On-Line
Public Records Office Vic. (p.31), 12800/PIH2888
State Library of NSW (p.11), GPO 1-31931
State Library of Victoria (pp. 7, 12, 13, 14, 77) A/508/08/172, H83-319, VAN15/09/88/172,
                                         H99.201/3120, H98.301/2098
State Library South Australia (pp.13, 34), B10212/12, PRG280/1/32/24
Hohner Museum (Martin Haffner) Germany

Thanks to the associates and friends who have helped over the years with information and photos:
Neil Brinsmead
Bruce Burgoyne
Peter Burgis (Australian Institute of Recorded Sound)
The Campbell family
The Collier family
Harland Crain and Doug Dawson (SPAH)
Donald Crombie
Ian Cummings
The Late Horrie Dargie
John Edmonds
The Late Ron Gerrard
Trevor Griffiths
Stu Hunter
J. Albert & Son "Boomerang Budget"
The Late Kurt Jacob (Hohner Australia)
The Late Harry Kay
The Late Sue Kelly
The Leeman family

National Film & Sound Archive Canberra (Nick Weare)
Ronald Omond
Arnold Percy
Greg Reeves
Jac and Tricia Smits (Smits Music)
The South Street Eisteddfod Society Ballarat
The Late George Ramage
The Late Bruce Skurray
The Late Harry Thompson
Kim Van Dokkum
The Late Eddie Wakefield
The Late Doug Wallace

Pat Missin - renowned harmonica musician, author and researcher of the U.K., has for some time been studying the origins of the instrument through patent applications and trademarks. His work in this area has recently resulted in the discovery of a patent from 1908 by Australian, Sydney Dickens, for a 'mouth organ attachment'. (See page 43).
Pat's discovery would indicate that Mr. Sydney Dickens was the 'Professor Dickens' featured on recordings made c. 1908 in Australia.

Phil Sheppard (Shep) - Melbourne harmonicist and presenter of the former Harmonica Riff-Raff radio program and now Blog, has delved further into the lives of some of the mouth organ players from my books, as well as a search for other rare 'Australian brand-name' harmonicas.
The results have been more than worthwhile and along the way he managed to add one of the world's most rare harmonicas to his collection.

Also Thanks to
Pam Merrigan and the National Folk Festival Canberra ACT
Bob Bolton, also the Late John Meredith AM, OAM and The Bush Music Club

Artwork, restoration and enhancement of harmonica illustrations by Raema Grieve

A special thank you to Rhianne Grieve and Lyall Grieve.

The author of the poem, "Australia's Own" on Page One - Chapter One of this book has not been identified, though some have suggested that it was penned by C.J. Dennis.

Introduction

After the publication by Currency Press of my first book, "A Band in a Waistcoat Pocket" in 1995, I was left with files still full of unfinished stories, unpublished photographs and pieces of information that I felt warranted exposure, not only for harmonica aficionados, collectors and players, but for those who have a general interest in Australian music history.

Therefore this new book, "Boomerangs and Crackajacks", provides many more details about the early years of the harmonica in Australia. In some cases, this emerged from simply dusting off the above-mentioned files but in the thirty years since my initial research began, computer technology has changed drastically; archival information that would have taken days, months or even longer to uncover could now be accessed in a much shorter space of time. In fact, some of my new research efforts became almost too easy by comparison!

My experience in documenting this history has been rewarding on a personal basis. Lots of new harmonica activity has taken place, with the return of a few harmonica sections included in local eisteddfods and contests, as well as a growing interest by collectors world-wide, in Australian harmonicas. The decision by the Seydel Company in Germany to once again resume manufacture of the Boomerang mouth organ after my continuous requests for information in the 1980s was certainly a highlight! (I hope Frank Albert would have approved). Another highlight for me was to be asked to act as an adjudicator at the Sydney Harmonica Championship in 2001, organised by John McDougall of the Woodstock Harmonica Association. Fortunately, I was not alone in this duty, sharing it with two local legends: Jim Conway, Australia's foremost blues harp player and Kim Van Dokkum, South Australian soloist and leader of the Harmonicaires in the 1950s and 1960s. Meanwhile, the harmonica magazines of John McDougall ("Woodstock") and Hohner's Tricia Smits ("Harpoz"), kept everyone informed.

I discovered some time later that the CD collection of the old-time players that I had released with the book had been used on occasions at the funeral services of those who had played and loved the mouth organ for much of their lives. Some of the more famous or well-known players have sadly, also passed on, including Lionel Easton, Richard Brooks, Horrie Dargie and Hohner's Kurt Jacob. Their friendship and the help they gave me with my research will always be appreciated. Kurt became a mentor to many players on his arrival in Australia in the 1930s, when the Hohner brand was enjoying unprecedented popularity, thanks in part to Larry Adler, (also no longer with us) and was held in the highest regard by all. At Kurt's funeral, I noticed Richard Brooks discreetly place a small Hohner harmonica on his coffin just before the service ended and I realised what strong bonds so many of the players of that era must have shared.

Their time has passed but the instrument was reborn decades ago when modern blues and rock emerged and the mouth organ gave new inspiration and pleasure as the blues harp. New music has been played, new bonds have been formed and new stories have been told by another generation of players. "Boomerangs and Crackajacks" takes another look at how it all started.

Ray Grieve 2014

Chapter One

A Very Early Arrival

"Australia's Own"
Circa 1927

Let the trombone player blow,
Let the fiddler scrape his bow,
Let the 'cello and the viol do their worst,
But the Aussie knocks 'em blue,
Has the mouth to do it too,
And the mouth organ has put Australia first.

Some prefer an oboe tune,
Flute, piano or bassoon,
The mouth organ is the dinkum Aussie's joy,
All are drowned you will allow,
In the glad uproarious row,
When he starts to raise "The Wild Colonial Boy".

Fugues and solos in D flat,
Bach, Beethoven and all that,
Are all right on swell violas of swanky tone,
But then you should hear the vamp,
Of the Barcoo Cattle Camp,
On the mouth organ which is Australia's own.

You should hear his zeal and zest,
At some country dance out west,
Never mind the soft pp and soulful sigh,
But his healthy lungs expand,
And he'd drown a piper's band,
When he strikes up "On The Road To Gundagai".

Let them finger flats and sharps,
On their highbrow lyres and harps,
Let them barrack for the organ deep and grand,
Let them praise the skirling pipes,
But for melody, by cripes,
You can't beat the way Australia beats the band.

"Glugs"

2   BOOMERANGS AND CRACKAJACKS

The story of the harmonica in Australia began with the importation by retail traders of small quantities of Austrian and German-manufactured instruments. They arrived by sail in Sydney from Europe and were usually thought of as toys before gradually gaining a wider acceptance and popularity over a number of years.

With the advent of the gold-rushes and the growing popularity of vaudeville, it became much more familiar on a national level by the 1870s.

Four Australian International Exhibitions held between 1879 and 1889 saw a huge increase in the importation of all varieties of goods including harmonicas. Germany by this time was the leading harmonica manufacturer supplying world markets such as America and Britain with their own brand-names. Australia followed this trend with the German-manufactured Woolloomooloo Warbler and Kangaroo Charmer models which came on the market via J. Albert & Son in 1896.

It would bring great satisfaction to know who brought the first harmonicon into Australia. A free-settler or perhaps even a prisoner in chains who was almost certainly unaware of his role, would have arrived in the British-ruled convict-colony (with a European population of around fifty thousand), after a journey of many months. After alighting from his ship at Sydney Cove he would have walked up a dusty or mud-filled George or Pitt Street, presumably carrying one in his pocket. Jewish merchant, Abraham Polack doesn't quite fit the above imagined scenario but he could well have been that elusive history-maker, though he did it on a slightly larger scale.

Polack (1797-1873), had small warehouses or shops from which he sold the goods he had imported from Europe to private individuals, distributors or retailers. He moved to different locations around the northern end of Sydney Town and over the following years became a very successful auctioneer and land-owner, until some dubious business dealings resulted in his imprisonment for some time. While trading at 7 Pitt Street, he advertised his wares as usual in "The Sydney Gazette and NSW Advertiser", the following occasion being on June 2$^{nd.}$ 1825. He stated that he had a range of assorted goods for sale. They consisted of: *'canisters of gunpowder, calico and scented soap, sheep shears, coffee, tea, pots, penknives, combs and razors, ladies gloves and writing paper'* etc. Also on the list were *'mouth organs of all descriptions'*.

Polack had placed another advertisement in the same paper six months before on the 24th November 1824, under the heading, *'Christmas Comes But Once A Year'*, claiming that he had for sale *'the largest investment of toys ever imported into the Colony'*. They included: *'fiddles, flutes, fifes, trumpets, drums, tambourines'* and *'many other articles consisting of different inventions'*.

It is possible that the 'articles consisting of different inventions' referred to the very latest invention of the time, the mouth organ, unfamiliar to everyone including Polack himself. This shipment would have left Europe sometime around the middle of 1824.

It might also be possible to suggest the brand-names of the 'mouth organs of all descriptions' as advertised by Polack. Martin Haffner and Hans Lindenmuller have undertaken extensive research into this formerly unknown area of the early manufacturers for their book *"Harmonica Makers of Germany and Austria"* (Published c.2003 Germany).

They have revealed that Georg Anton Reinlein was producing and distributing harmonicas from Austria in 1824-1825 and they discovered some evidence that two craftsmen, Johann Langhammer in Bohemia and C. W. Meisel in Klingenthal might have been producing such instruments in 1823. This would suggest that Polack's mouth organs consisted of at least one of these brands.

Over the following decade, most of the shipments that arrived were described as toys. In December of 1828, Mr Deane of Bartholomew Fair in Elizabeth Street Hobart announced in the "Hobart Town Courier", that he 'had just opened a case of toys of great variety' which included mouth organs.

Perhaps Deane was selling the same brands as Polack had sold in Sydney two years before, but by now a few more manufacturers had begun making and distributing mouth organs.

Christian Messner of Trossingen was one of these. He would begin a long tradition of harmonica-making in the German town. Joseph Richter in Bohemia was said to have started production also by this time. His name would live on as the one who eventually 'reconfigured' the instrument from its toy status by the development of a new tuning system.

The Austrian and German harmonica-makers might have been pleased to know that on the other side of the world, some of the residents of Sydney Town were discovering the pleasure and confidence the little instrument could bring, especially after taking a few drinks.

The 'jig was up' for Sydney Smith in May of 1831, when he downed some liquor and danced his way through the streets of the Town playing "Drops O' Brandy" on his mouth organ. He was arrested for disturbing the peace by being *'drunk and riotous'* and fined five shillings. Smith and his mouth organ solo performance had accidentally made the news, probably the first time for the instrument in Australia, when his charge was reported in "The Sydney Herald" of May the 30th.

Another report a few years later in June 1833, showed that Smith was not alone in this type of activity. Three men, William Ball, William Horden and Arthur Parr were arrested late on a Wednesday night in a Sydney street, on a charge of *'vagabondism and for dancing a seraband to music pulled out of a mouth organ'*. The mouth organ trio were later released without charges.

It was only a month later, when reports of an interesting duo act featuring the instrument, appeared on the streets of Sydney Town.

Charles and Ann Mahony were arrested and charged with the following:

'Rolling through the public streets at night, he playing on a mouth organ and she screeching in concert'.

The Hobart docks were busy in December 1834 with the usual arrivals of convict ships, while among the merchant ship arrivals were the "Janet" and the "Eveline", carrying passengers and goods of all kinds from London. Some of the goods were imported by W. Carter of Derwent House in Elizabeth Street, Hobart, (opposite the "Ship Inn"). They included cases of homeware, clothing and furniture.
In the "Hobart Town Courier", Carter announced that: *'The recent importations by the "Janet" and the "Eveline" from London are now open and consist of a choice selection of summer goods.'*
They also included a selection of toys:
'Noahs arks and animals, cricket bats and balls, humming tops, looking glasses, whistles and masks and mouth organs'.
Carter might have had a much more extensive range in stock than the previously mentioned sellers. Haffner and Lindenmuller in *"Harmonica Makers of Germany and Austria"* have listed many more manufacturers who were active now, and noticeably include quite a few small Austrian workshops.
They were Johannes Fell, Vincenz Fischer, Joseph Forstner, Michael Hartig, Jacob Kissling and Wilhelm Thie who would soon become one of the world's biggest harmonica makers.
In Germany, Friedrich Hotz was becoming well-established along with Johannes Bilger, both of Knittlingen. Johann Wilhelm Glier of Klingenthal was also producing the instrument.

The newspapers of the day mention imports that continued throughout the 1830s: *'An assortment of new and useful goods including Superior Music Boxes (4 and 6 tunes), musical snuff-boxes, coloured playing-cards and mouth organs 3d. to 1/6d.*
James Maclehose, Hunter Street Sydney ("Sydney Gazette and NSW Advertiser", 13th June 1837).
In Van Diemen's Land, Boon and Co. of 40 Elizabeth Street Hobart stated: *'We respectfully inform the public that we have just received and opened three cases of toys which contain as under:*
'Whips with whistles, dissected alphabets, harmonicons and Jews harps with a great variety of tin and other toys'. ("Hobart Town Courier", 16th June 1837).
J.W. Davis had *'gigs, horses, omnibus, tumblers and balance horses, barking dogs, hand and mouth organs'.* ("Hobart Town Courier", 22nd September 1837).

About eighteen months later, the mouth harmonicon or harmonica as it was now sometimes called (and not to be confused with a separate instrument, the glass harmonica), came under the hammer at Mr Blackman's Auction and Commission Rooms, Regent Terrace, Hunter Street Sydney:
"The Sydney Gazette and NSW Advertiser" reported that three cases of toys were up for auction, their contents including panoramas, puzzles, rattles and mouth organs.

The annual 'Fancy Fair', under the patronage of Lady Franklin, wife of The Governor, His Excellency Sir John Franklin, was held at the Argyle Rooms in Hobart Town. This event was a fundraiser for the Infant School Society and one of the popular social events that always drew a huge crowd.

Lady Franklin was much admired for having brought culture from England to the convict isle and was active in Hobart society, lending her name to charity groups and other organisations. In 1838 all manner of goods were on sale at the Fair, including toys such as Dutch leather and wax dolls with moving eyes, bows and arrows, boxing gloves, magnetic and silver fishes, drums, Pandean pipes and mouth organs. The 21st Regiment Band supplied the music for the day.

Pioneer of Australian theatre, Barnett Levy opened the first 'legitimate' theatre in Australia in 1833. A controversial figure, Levy and his Theatre Royal in George Street, Sydney, enjoyed a short and turbulent history before he died in 1837 and the Royal was destroyed by fire in 1840. The harmonica made the news in a negative, though humorous manner once again, this time in a rumour that went around town in early 1834, concerning Levy's theatre. The story was that Levy was having disagreements with the management concerning the Theatre Royal Orchestra, probably regarding costs among other things and due to this, the Orchestra had been reduced in number to a kettle-drum and a mouth organ!

Four years later, in Sydney in 1838 at the new Royal Victoria Theatre in Pitt Street, a 'mythological, musical burlesque burletta' by Mr Joseph Greaves Esq. entitled "Cupid" and starring Miss Lazar, played on Tuesday the 18th September. "Cupid" had previously enjoyed considerable success in London.

One of the visiting cast members was the actor and dancer, Mr Hollis who played Pan. He had been described as 'a Professor of Music and a Paganini of the Mouth Organ'.

Just what was required of Hollis in the play, to execute such a performance on an instrument that had some limitations in 1838, can only be imagined. Perhaps some 'special-effects' or comedy style of playing was needed.

No one could have guessed in 1838, that a century later, a term such as 'Paganini of the Mouth Organ' would no longer be considered a joke, and that the once humble harmonica would be taken very seriously.

The Royal Victoria Theatre.
Sydney venue for "Pan" in 1838

Whenever thoughts turn to harmonicas, the song "Home, Sweet Home" always seems to come to mind. At least this was the case for around one hundred years or so.

It could be said that both the instrument and the song were conceived and then presented to the public in the same years.

While the Austrian and German craftsmen were experimenting with simple prototypes of mouth harmonicas in 1821, Englishman, Henry Rowley Bishop was discovering a European traditional patriotic air from some music he had been commissioned to edit.

Henry Bishop was a composer, arranger and conductor of high-renown who was eventually knighted for his achievements in music. Inspired by the piece, he wrote a song for inclusion in his forthcoming opera, "Clari, or the Maid of Milan", with words added by well-known American actor, poet and playwright, John Howard Payne, who was living in England at the time. Payne's achievements include his studies of Native American cultures, and government appointments to North Africa.

"Clari, the Maid of Milan" opened in 1823, possibly the year that the first harmonicas were sold commercially and although the opera was soon forgotten, the 'song' was considered a great success and published in its own right soon after, as "Home, Sweet Home".

So great was the success of "Home, Sweet Home" that it would be eventually described as the most famous song ever written.

The ease with which a song of relatively few notes such as "Home, Sweet Home" could be played on a single-key small instrument such as the harmonica, soon made it a favourite for players who discovered the instrument over the next few decades.

The melancholic and haunting sound of the instrument made a perfect match and an instrumental substitute for Payne's equally melancholic lyrics. As playing ability and technique with vibrato and other effects improved, the song could still be given its full meaning and effect.

The American Civil War in the 1860s saw the real consummation of instrument and song in the eyes of most people, even those outside of America itself.

The song was a favourite on both sides of the battle, inspiring images that have become legends: the homesick soldier playing "Home, Sweet Home" on his harmonica.

One of the many outcomes of such legends was a stage-play based around the Civil War, introduced in 1873 and starring Mr and Mrs J. C. Williamson, (the latter being his wife, Maggie Moore). The play, "Struck Oil" was very successful in England, prompting the Williamsons to take the production around the world.

Opening in Australia in 1874, Maggie Moore's performance had local audiences in raptures, resulting in her becoming one the most popular and most-loved actors in local theatre history. It also happened that one of the most admired segments of the play was her performance on the mouth organ of "Home, Sweet Home"

"Struck Oil" concerned the story of the Dutch Stofel family in America amidst the Civil War and the discovery of oil.
Maggie Moore played Lizzie Stofel and James Williamson played her father John, a cobbler. The play consisted of three acts and contained six songs and dances. Moore's acting role required a Dutch accent with which she captivated audiences, as did her singing and dancing routine.
The Civil War saw John Stofel leave and return a broken man and the touching scene where Lizzie plays "Home, Sweet Home" on the mouth organ for him had an emotional impact on Australian theatre goers.

The Williamsons in "Struck Oil"
(Lizzie Stofel and her mouth organ)

With the phenomenal success of "Struck Oil", the Williamsons toured the world as planned, making many visits back to Australia, which they eventually called 'home'.
Maggie Moore, born in 1851, had a local connection. Her mother and family moved from Ireland and lived briefly in Australia before settling in America.
The Williamsons were divorced by 1899 and James went on to eventually lay the foundations of one of Australia's greatest theatre companies. Maggie Moore continued to tour "Struck Oil" internationally, just as successfully this time around with new husband and actor H.H. (Harry) Roberts. The following 1911 reviews appeared in "The Adelaide Advertiser":
-*'A good many years have passed since the talented actress originally played Lizzie Stofel in "Struck Oil" in Adelaide, but they have not impaired the winsome charm and sunny-hearted grace of Miss Moore's little Dutch girl who plays "Home, Sweet Home" on the mouth organ and sings farewell to her father in tones that vibrate straight to the hearts of the audience'.*
-*'Her rendering of "Home, Sweet Home" on a mouth organ is also an exceedingly clever and entertaining performance'.*

"Struck Oil" the movie, was made in Australia in 1920 starring Moore and Roberts and although it could never come close to equalling the success of the play, it was considered to be 'artistically acted and produced and very well received'.
("The Argus" 22nd March 1920).
Maggie Moore died as the result of a cable-car accident in San Francisco in 1926.

Maggie Moore

Within a few months of the Williamsons' performances of "Struck Oil", the famous American artist, Joseph K. Emmet arrived in 1876 for a stay which would last nearly two years and include a brief visit to New Zealand.

Born in 1841 in St. Louis, Emmet had developed a Dutch/German song and dance comedy routine in his early career around 1866, while working in vaudeville. Predominantly English-speaking audiences found the European accent a novelty and Emmet enjoyed huge success, especially from 1869 when he developed a German alter-ego called 'Fritz'. A big reason for the success of "Struck Oil" was due to the German/Dutch accents of the characters, particularly Maggie Moore's little Dutch girl, Lizzie Stofel who played "Home, Sweet Home" on the mouth organ. It would appear that "Struck Oil" and many other plays overseas were very much inspired by Emmet's 'Fritz'.

Emmet encountered a problem from the beginning of his visit which was directly related to "Struck Oil" and the success the play had achieved in Australia. Emmet wrote a play with music titled "Fritz, Our Cousin German" which he performed in Australia with a cast of around twelve, a large local group of extras, and a small orchestra. On opening, unfortunate comparisons were made to "Struck Oil", the comment being that perhaps audiences were tiring of the Dutch/German accent novelty, (not realising at the time that "Struck Oil" would continue to be played in Australia successfully for decades to come).

After a short while however, the Emmet play drew huge crowds although this seemed to be equally due to the gradual realisation of his talent as a musician as well as his acting, dancing and singing abilities. "Fritz, Our Cousin German" was accepted as a vehicle for these talents rather than as a production in its own right. Emmet the musician greatly impressed local audiences and critics: *'He plays the guitar as no one else who has appeared in this city has played it'* - *'He is a master of the banjo'* - *'plays the drum exceedingly well'*, (referring to an American Coin Silver Drum which had been presented to him by his friends in St. Louis) and *'does more with the mouth harmonicon than anyone else has done'*. ("The Argus" 27th March 1876). "The Australasian Sketcher" also gave an impressive review, stating that 'when playing that modern Pandean pipe, the mouth harmonicon, he is an adept and brings out of that unpromising instrument, combinations of sounds that could hardly have been expected.'

Emmet's harmonicon playing introduced a brand new and exciting progression in the instrument for Australians with German-accented advertisements for his shows announcing that on 'dot toy harmonic' (that toy harmonica), 'he has no equal' and plays 'five distinct variations of "Home, Sweet Home."' The five variations were obviously the steps that would become the accepted way to learn the instrument in the coming years: single notes, chords and tremolo, vibrato and cupped- hand positions.

This display of the new way to play the mouth organ left audiences amazed and was a demonstration by Emmet that his "Home, Sweet Home" was much more impressive than Maggie Moore's basic interpretation in "Struck Oil".

Left:
Joseph K. Emmet
Above:
The Genuine Joseph Emmet Richter harmonica

Emmet's success as 'Fritz' continued internationally, although his Australian visit was marred to some degree by bouts of odd behaviour, said to have been the result of a drinking problem. At one of his Melbourne performances, which was attended by His Excellency the Governor, Sir George Bowen, he fell over several times during a dance segment and shortly after, fell fast asleep in the middle of a sketch. The curtains were drawn, the management made apologies and patrons were given tickets for the following night's show. One reporter commented that 'he had obviously indulged too freely in his country's primest whiskey'.

Another example occurred while Emmet was staying at the Pier Hotel in the Adelaide seaside suburb of Glenelg, with his wife and young son. "The Sydney Morning Herald" on the 7th August 1877, reported that early one evening he was seen to: *'leave the hotel, leap over the sea wall, rush madly along the beach and plunge into the sea. He was enveloped in an Ulster overcoat at the time and on getting into the water, he rolled over on his back, making the most frantic movements.'* He was at once followed by one of the hotel barmen and was eventually dragged out with the help of a nearby fisherman. Upon reaching dry land *'Mr. Emmet gave vent to a hearty peal of laughter'*. Back at the hotel shortly after, he was heard *'amusing himself by playing a few tunes on the mouth harmonicon'*.

It was said that Emmet had behaved in exactly the same way on another occasion, but his agent quickly issued a statement claiming that the story was wrong and that he had simply gone for swim, an activity he enjoyed. Back in New York, he was gaoled briefly in 1880 after a charge was brought against him by his wife and son concerning his drinking habits. He died of pneumonia in New York in 1891. His visit was long remembered by Australians and there is no doubt that his harmonica expertise introduced new and exciting possibilities for future players. From press reports he was also a pioneer in guitar techniques, an instrument that would also become immensely popular in modern music.

Vaudeville shows and individual performers from America and England kept arriving on Australia's shores over the years with more advertisements claiming new clever and amazing effects on mouth organs as well as those five variations of "Home, Sweet Home".

10 BOOMERANGS AND CRACKAJACKS

The invention of the telephone by Alexander Graham Bell, first displayed in America in 1876, soon became one of the main topics of interest and conversation around the world, particularly in isolated Australia with the possibility that it might eventually replace the Morse Code system of communication.

On 12th January 1878, the New South Wales Telegraph Department decided to try out Bell's new telephone invention by making up a crude version of their own and testing it in Sydney. "The Sydney Morning Herald" of 14th January, explained that they had constructed instruments based on Bell's design, setting one up in the city and the other in the suburb of La Perouse, about fifteen kilometres distance, on the shores of Botany Bay. Superintendent Mr E. Cracknell and Superintendent Taylor of the New Zealand cable were at the La Perouse end, while Mr Wilson and Mr Gustavo Kopech, both of the Department, manned the city site. Kopech worked as a telegraph electrician at concerts and functions at the Exhibition Buildings in Sydney's Prince Alfred Park. The experiment started with a verbal conversation after which Kopech played a tune on a harmonicon and a bugle, followed by Taylor with two vocal efforts: "We Sat by the River, You and I" and "Little Footsteps."

The historic 'first Australian telephone-call-experiment' was proclaimed a great success with a perfect reception received, the harmonicon (and bugle), coming through loud and clear.

The mouth harmonicon, (harmonica or mouth organ), was certainly becoming more familiar with Australians but not everyone was impressed, judging by the poem below that was doing the rounds in the 1880s and penned by a sufferer who complained that the sound of the harmonicon was responsible for the death of his cat!

A young man near my humble cot,
Plays on the low harmonicon
All through summer evenings hot
He plays and plays and then plays

And as he played my Thomas cat
Would listen - 'twas in years gone by
Would listen with his ears laid flat
And love-light kindling in his eye

He thought it was a feline voice
Of some Maria in the spheres
And that is why he would rejoice
And horizontal lay his ears

He pined for her who never lived
He pined and of the pine he died
His soul to death he gently gived
With just one sigh unsatisfied

He died. Beside my neighbour's door
One eve I placed my wasted pet
I wail a cat who wails no more
But the harmonicon wails yet.

In 1872, Melbourne tailor John Williamson became aware that the mouth organ was gaining popularity and used the instrument in this advertisement to lure young men into his shop to buy a suit

READ YE DYSPEPTICS.— Facts stranger than Fiction.— One shilling. A Musical Box, carriage included It stamps; playing eight select airs, charming tones and brilliant action, full size, in handsome polished wood case, metal tongues and plates, new patented pattern, genuine durable article, suitable for all; in proof of which we guarantee each box, and will at once return the stamps where complete satisfaction is not given. You may depend there were many dupes. How different the manner of advertisements carried out at Melbourne House, St. Kilda. The musical box was what is called a mouth organ, it was necessarily of the keyless pattern for there were no works to be wound up, and if you could play on it at all you might play any number of select airs. It was also said to be eminently adapted for the drawing-room, that was a matter of opinion: however, it had a large sale, especially amongst boys, who carried misery into many a quiet home, but all this is compensated for by JOHN WILLIAMSON, of Melbourne House, Tailor, High-street, St. Kilda, who strikes his customers into an ecstacy of joy when he shows them what Suits he makes to their measure for 50s., all wool, and shrunk. Give him a call ye dyspeptics.—ALFE

Left:
The Austrian Court at the 1879 Sydney International Exhibition.

Below:
Award-Winning Wilhelm Thie instruments and medal

The decade of the International Exhibitions ushered in a new era for many Australians. The first was the Sydney event, which opened in 1879.

For the first time, they could gaze at the lifestyle, art, culture, craftsmanship and machinery of Europe, displayed in impressive and beautifully decorated settings. The harmonicon played a very small part in all of this, but it surprised the visitor in more ways than one. This 'foreign little instrument' as many thought of it, was not just a toy or vaudeville comedy prop, but now also a thing of great quality and exceptional craftsmanship, something they could well appreciate. They looked in awe at the display cases of Viennese manufacturer Wilhelm Thie, one of the world's biggest harmonica-makers. The Wilhelm Thie display was awarded a Silver Medal.

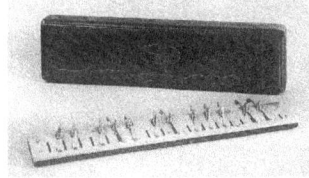

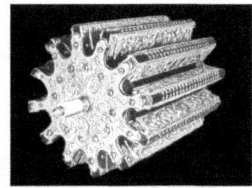

12 BOOMERANGS AND CRACKAJACKS

*Austrian exhibits being unloaded from the S.S. "Polluce" in Melbourne for the 1880 Melbourne International Exhibition
Below:
Austrian Court at the Melbourne International Exhibition with Award-Winning Medal and Wilhelm Thie harmonicons*

With the Melbourne International Exhibition held shortly after the closure of the Sydney event in 1880, many items were temporarily stored, then shipped to Melbourne for display.

The Wilhelm Thie display again impressed the public, the press and the judges who awarded a Silver Medal to the Austrian manufacturer.

Trimmel and Zettl, also from Vienna, exhibited display cases of various harmonicons. Friedrich Hotz of Knittlengen represented the German manufacturers with twenty one harmonicons.

*Wilhelm Thie
First Order of Merit
Silver Medal 1880*

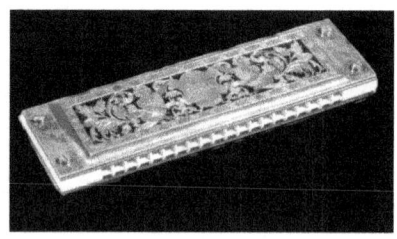

The German Court at the 1880 Melbourne International Exhibition

The Award Presentation Ceremony at the 1880 Melbourne International Exhibition

At the Adelaide International Exhibition of 1887, Wilhelm Thie once again exhibited an array of fine quality harmonicas. No awards were given for harmonicas at this event.

The Austrian Court at the 1887 Adelaide International Exhibition

14 BOOMERANGS AND CRACKAJACKS

The Wilhelm Thie Factory did not enter a display in the 1888 Melbourne Centennial Exhibition; instead Austria was represented by P.H. Brunnbauer, also of Vienna, a much smaller manufacturer though one that was renowned for the very highest quality hand-crafted instruments.

There could have been a personal reason for this. It was suggested to the author in correspondence many years ago from Otto Thie, a family descendant, that this may have been a deliberate move by Wilhelm, son of Wilhelm Snr., the original founder.

Phillip Brunnbauer was a close family friend and mentor to Wilhelm Jnr. and was in fact Godfather to one of his sons. Otto Thie suggested that perhaps Wilhelm Thie did not want to compete with Brunnbauer for sales (and possibly awards) at this particular time and so was not part of the 1888 Exhibition. Otto Thie also advised that this was speculation and might not have been the actual reason.

It was a successful enterprise for Brunnbauer however, who was awarded a Silver Medal for his impressive display of high-quality harmonicons.

Also from Austria was H. Trapp of Nuekirchen with a display case of various harmonicon and from Germany, the C.H. Weiss Harmonica Factory of Trossingen, one of the world's big harmonica manufacturers of the period.

1888 Melbourne Centennial International Exhibition medal and Award–Winning P.H. Brunnbauer harmonica

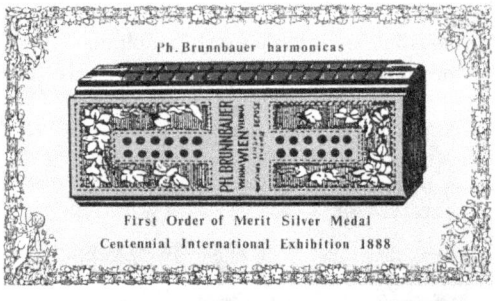

First Order of Merit Silver Medal Centennial International Exhibition 1888

Austrian Court: 1888 Melbourne Centennial International Exhibition

German Court: 1888 Melbourne Centennial International Exhibition

A VERY EARLY ARRIVAL 15

German harmonicas commemorating the
Australian International Exhibitions
Left: Ernst Leiterd (for Sydney 1879)
Below: Richter (for Melbourne 1880)

Right:
A collage of
advertisements
for Ernest Hosking's
appearances at the
Tasmanian
International
Exhibition in
Hobart in 1895.
Hosking was the
holder of three gold
medals, awarded by
the Governor-General
Lord Linlithgow for
his mouth organ and
magic performances.

16 BOOMERANGS AND CRACKAJACKS

The Royal Agricultural Show

A NEW MOUTH ORGAN.

Messrs. W. F. Coxon and Co. have something remarkably original in a new mouth organ called the "Lyre Bird." This mouth organ is Mr. W. F. Coxon's invention, and is the result of years of experiment, having been tested and found perfect. The opinion of experts who have seen it is that there is nothing better. The reeds are filed vertically and diagonally, thus giving the true and correct tone; a splendid ornamental, plush-lined case is provided with each instrument. It was awarded special prize at the Agricultural Society's show, 1903.

The ingenuity of Australians has once more made itself conspicuous; this time in the invention of a mouth organ called the Lyre Bird, by Mr. W. F. Coxon, of the firm W. F. Coxon and Company, Limited, Haymarket, Sydney. This invention has been perfected after years of study. The reeds are made of "bell metal alloy," the same as used in making the great cathedral bells of the world. Each part is detachable, and can be replaced when worn out. An ornamental plush-lined case is provided with each instrument, which has been awarded special prize at Agricultural Society's Show, 1903.

An original and strikingly well-finished mouth organ has come to hand from Messrs. W. F. Coxon and Co., Ltd., Haymarket, called the "Lyre Bird," and invented by Mr. W. F. Coxon, who has been many years persevering to bring this mouth organ to perfection. The reeds are made of the very best material obtainable by a special reed maker, who has devoted his whole life to the making and perfecting of sonorous sounding reeds, and these are the only kind used in the "Lyre Bird." Every instrument is warranted true and correct in tone, and they are sure to grow popular. Each instrument is provided with a handsome plush-lined case. Awarded special prize at the Agricultural Society's Show, 1903.

The Lyre Bird 1903-1910

Moore Park Sydney 1903

COXON'S MOUTH ORGAN CONTEST, to be held in the Forrester's Hall, corner of Darby and Church sts., DECEMBER 23rd, 1904, at 8 p.m. First prize, Silver Cup; Second Prize, Silver Watch; Third Prize, One of Coxon's Accordeons. Entrance Fee 6d. For information see handbills, and at
   COXON'S SHOP,
   151 Hunter-st. W.

Last night, in the Oddfellows' Hall, Lower Church-street, a mouth organ contest was conducted, the instruments used being Coxon's lyrebird mouth organs. There was a fair attendance, and the audience expressed appreciation of the efforts of the players. There were nine contestants, and each exhibited much skill in evolving music from the small instruments. In the first round A. J. Stollery, W. Ferrer, and Edward Parkes were each awarded 50 points. In the second round Stollery, who played splendidly, was placed first with 55 points, total 105; Ferrer second, 50 points, total 100; and Parkes third with 45 points, total 95. The first prize was a silver cup, the second a silver watch, and the third an accordion. They were awarded by W. F. Coxon and Co. Ltd.

Chapter Two

Australian by Name

According to a reporter at one of the International Exhibitions of the 1880s, the mouth organ was an instrument that was familiar to most Australians. This statement is borne out by the fact that when competitions were held, harmonica sections were often featured and amateur social bands included them, sometimes as novelty instruments, although more increasingly as time went on, as a legitimate part of the line-up. The following story from the "Brisbane Courier" in 1886 is just one example:

The Queensland Football Club band had a 'mouth harmonicon' in their outfit and 'two tin whistles (in the same key), two cornets, a flute, the bones and a vocal chorus'. The band was made up from the team players and was dubbed "The Egmont Band" after the steamer, "Egmont" on which they travelled down south to compete (unsuccessfully as it turned out), in inter-colonial matches against New South Wales football teams in Sydney and Newcastle. The Band played with great gusto as the "Egmont" left Brisbane in June of 1886, down the Brisbane River and out into the Pacific. Unfortunately, they experienced very heavy weather and rough seas, resulting in complete musical silence, however much less pleasant sounds were heard for the three days that they rocked and rolled their way down the coast and into Sydney Heads. The newspaper reported however, that once inside the Heads, "The Egmont Band" was once again heard *'in full-blast'*.

After a week or so of matches, smoke concerts and receptions, including a formal welcome by the Mayor of Sydney, the Queensland Football Team returned home on the "Ranelagh". They had a fast and pleasant trip and it comes as no surprise to learn just what tune the Band was playing when they reached the Brisbane Wharf: that well-established favourite of the time, "Home, Sweet Home".

There would be many more renditions of "Home, Sweet Home" heard all over Australia from 1896, when J. Albert & Son of King Street Sydney, introduced the first 'home-brand-name' mouth organs. The Woolloomooloo Warbler and the Kangaroo Charmer, manufactured by Seydel & Son of Germany, one of the world's leading manufacturers, were an immediate success.

This seemed to be what many Australian players had been waiting for. In fact, a year before the Albert instruments had made their debut, a Police Magistrate in Brisbane, Mr Hill, had even invented his own mouth organ as told by the "Brisbane Courier" of January 7th 1895.

He was part of a group of amateur players who appeared before a large audience to raise funds for the local church. He played piano, sang a 'corroboree' and then played a selection on 'a kind of mouth organ that he had invented and made himself,' and which he had named 'the Jim-Jam.' "The Brisbane Courier" added that *'the instrument was very sweet-toned and the selection was much appreciated'*.

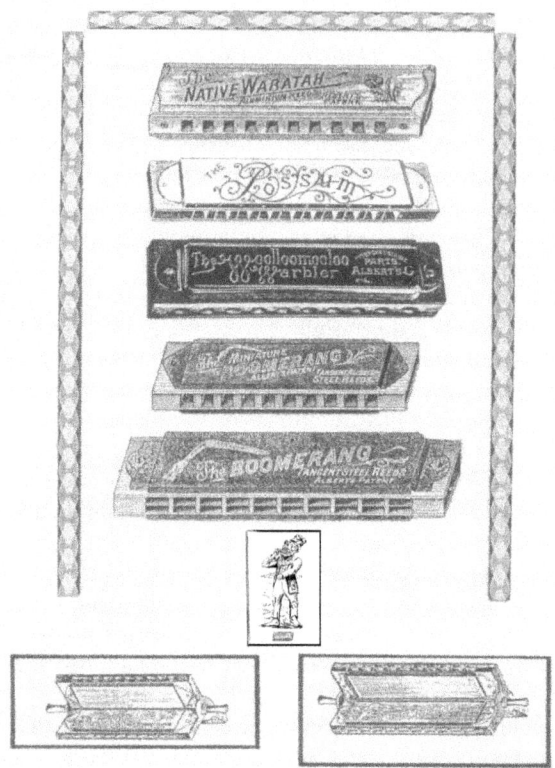

Australian brand-name mouth organs by J. Albert & Son 1896–1898
Native Waratah, Possum, Woolloomooloo Warbler, Boomerang Miniature,
Boomerang large, (King Billy advertisement),
3-sided Boomerang Miniature, 3-sided Boomerang large

For a few months after its introduction, the Woolloomooloo Warbler was advertised as featuring a 'patented bone lip-protector'. This feature was soon discontinued.

Late in 1896, the two-sided King Billy, the Boomerang large, Boomerang Miniature, Native Waratah, Wallaby and Possum models became available and in 1898, the Boomerang three-sided large and Boomerang three-sided Miniature followed. The Native Waratah featured a lip-protector and celluloid sliding covers.

In 1902 J. Albert & Son moved across to the other side of King Street and introduced the Boomerang Professional and the Boomerang Miniature Professional, both with metal lip-protectors. In the following years, the two-sided Boomerang large, two-sided Boomerang Miniature, three-sided Boomerang Professional, the Kookaburra and the Boomerang Pocket were made available. All Professional models and eventually, the Kookaburra were fitted with lip-protectors.

In 1902 J. Albert & Son also introduced the Moa in four types for the New Zealand market. These were twenty and forty-reed models with and without horns attached.

The Boomerang large was by now, sporting a slightly redesigned cover-plate.

By 1911 the high-quality Boomerang Grands appeared. These included the Grand and Miniature Grand, each available in the normal nickel-plate finish with gilt lettering or black enamel with gilt lettering. The two black models were discontinued after only a few years. Five Boomerang Professional Arch-Bell models with bell attachments were then introduced around 1912.

J. Albert & Son advertisement

Frank Albert at J. Albert & Son
137 King Street Sydney c.1912

Australia became a Commonwealth member in 1901 and among the hundreds of people who marched in Sydney from the city to Centennial Park for the Celebrations, was the Boys Brigade Harmonica Band. The Hohner Company issued a special-edition box with harmonicas from Germany, to celebrate the Federation and years later, the Hohner Young Australia harmonica was introduced in two sizes, selling for 1/3d. and 2/-.

This attractive harmonica featured an engraved illustration of the Australian flag, which in 1928 was brought to the attention of the Federal Government. Not long before this, the Government had passed a bill stating that foreign goods imported into Australia bearing the Australian flag or coat of arms which might be seen as a trade mark, would be prohibited. Some exceptions were made, but by the year's end, the Hohner Young Australia would be rarely seen again.

In 1902, George Clark Allan and Charles Tait of Allan and Co. in Melbourne, Australia's largest music-house, introduced the Crackajack which was available initially in three models. Walter Omond, the Australian Champion, promoted both the Boomerang and Crackajack brands and years later, ran a hotel and then a dental surgery, in Melbourne.

"I swallowed me mouth organ Doc!"
"Was it a Boomerang or a Crackajack?"
Walter Omond, dentist, gives his nephew Albert a check-up at his Melbourne surgery around 1915

J. Albert & Son advertisement

AUSTRALIAN BY NAME 21

*The Crackajack range 1902-1926.
Manufactured for Allan & Co.
By F.A. Bohm of Klingenthal, Germany*

Allan and Tait

Will Van Allen — 'The Musical Tramp'

22 BOOMERANGS AND CRACKAJACKS

The Boomerangs of J. Albert & Son were by far the big sellers in the period up to World War I, but the Crackajacks of Allan & Co. were not far behind.

A group of twelve boys from Adelaide's Our Boys Institute, a similar charitable organisation to the Boys Brigade, had briefly formed a Crackajack mouth organ band in 1904, less than two years after the instrument's introduction. The Crackajack's popularity in both band and solo playing kept growing. By this time a multitude of other brands were also on sale including all the well-known German models and those that had been 'named' for the American and English markets. Two such examples were the Silver Tone and the Solo Grand, which were available for around ten years or more.

In 1902 Australian advertisements, the Solo Grand was called 'the boy's delight', available in nickel or aluminium cases, *'in competent hands, capable of brightening many homes'*.

The English Bess O' Th' Barn range was popular in Australia, with sales inspired by the legendary band's visits from 1906 to 1911. The Besses O' Th' Barn were here as part of two touring programs that took in a number of countries in the region.

Bess O' Th' Barn mouth organs were advertised in three sizes at the time:

The 20-reed Concert Artist with mouth plate and metal case 3/- and 1/6d and 1/- respectively.

From Germany in 1911, came the Swastika, introduced many years before Adolf Hitler and the Nazi Party had claimed and brought disrepute to the name and symbol. It was available in four types in Australia:

The 40-reed Special sold for 3/6d., the 40 Reed for 2/6d., the 20-reed Special sold for 2/- and the 20 reed for 1/6d. A very high quality instrument, the Swastika featured hard alloy reeds which were 'accurately tuned and then minutely adjusted'. All models came in metal cases.

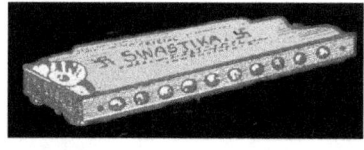

Advertisements proclaimed that 'the *Swastika charms every hearer. Rich and sonorous or light and bird-like, it permits of shades of expression and musical effects acceptable as much to the trained ear, as to the untutored listener'*.

Some of the other brands in the shops at the time included Hohner's Auto-Valve Harp, the double and single-sided National Band and Second-To-None and the Weiss Brass Band and Accordola, which was described as 'a striking novelty with chord and bass accompaniment'. 'While the melody is played in the normal manner, an accordion-like attachment supplies any series of chords desired'. Advertisements for the 40-steel-reed Bugler consoled parents by stating that the instrument produced a 'soft and mellow tone' for three shillings.

AUSTRALIAN BY NAME 23

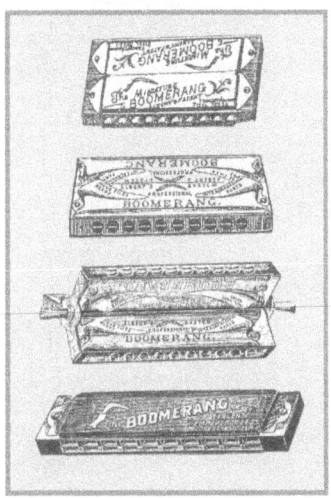

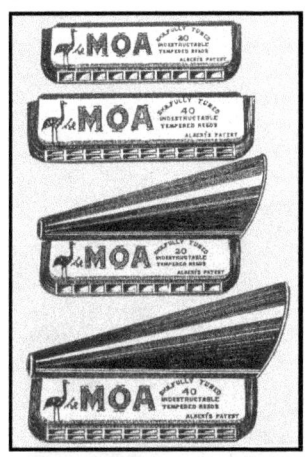

J. Albert & Son mouth organs from 1902:
Top left:
Boomerang Vest Pocket,
Boomerang Miniature Professional,
Boomerang Professional
Top right:
Moa 20-reed, Moa 40-reed,
Moaphone 20-reed, Moaphone 40-reed
Bottom left:
2-sided Boomerang Miniature,
2-sided Boomerang Professional,
3-sided Boomerang Professional,
Boomerang large
Bottom right:
Kookaburra with box

J. Albert & Son advertisement 1903

24 BOOMERANGS AND CRACKAJACKS

J. Albert & Son advertisement c.1904

Albert Boomerang mouth organs 1911-1912
Top Left:
Miniature Grand (nickel-plate)
Grand (nickel- plate)
Miniature Grand (black enamel)
Grand (black enamel)
Top Right:
Miniature Professional Arch-Bell
Professional Arch-Bell
Miniature Professional Arch-Bell double
2-sided Professional Arch-Bell
4-sided Professional Arch-Bell

Jackson and McDonald of Sydney introduced their mouth organ equivalent to the Boomerang and Crackajack in 1912. Called the Cobber, it was available in four types: the 40-reed Professional, 40-reed Standard, 20-reed Miniature Professional and 20-reed Vamper. The company, already well-known for its gramophone players and recordings, had a successful run with the Cobber, until it was discontinued around 1920.

The sales strategy for the new brand included a number of Cobber Mouth Organ Contests, held at suburban Sydney music shops and then in 1913, a New South Wales State Mouth Organ Championship Competition at the Glaciarium Theatre in Sydney with the inclusion of weekly limericks in "The Sunday Sun" newspaper. Written by Samuel Jackson, they were said to have been eagerly anticipated by the youngsters of the day.

The complete set of 1913 Cobber Mouth Organ Limericks is reproduced on the following pages.

"COBBER" MOUTH ORGAN CHAMPIONSHIP OF N.S. WALES.

WHAT MR. DONNELLY, THE CHAMPION, SAYS.

Mr. F. Donnelly was tutored by Albert Emmett, of Dr. Carver's Entertainers, America, 21 years ago. He later defeated Albert Emmett in a competition for a prize of £10, in 1908. Defeated S. Gardiner, the English champion, for a wager of £50 a side. Has appeared with Fuller's New Zealand Circuit, The Fredo Family, The Royal Burlesque Comedy Co., and The Matsa Vaudeville Co., in Australia and New Zealand. He holds the championships of Victoria and New Zealand, and has further added to his list of successes by winning the championship of New South Wales.

Mr. Donnelly says:—The "Cobber" on which I won the N.S.W. Championship I bought from Thomas and Co., Newtown, taking the first one they gave me. Every "Cobber" mouth organ I have had, and I have used no other for some time, has been perfectly satisfactory in every way. I am prepared to play any player who cares to challenge me, or refutes my right to hold the titles mentioned in this report, and the instrument that I will use will be a "Cobber."

What Mr. J. DONELLY the winner of the Cobber Mouth Organ Championship of New South Wales at Wests' Glaciarium and numerous other championships says. "I am quite convinced that the Cobber Mouth Organ is the Best I Have Ever Played

James Donnelly (b. USA 1865) visited Australia and New Zealand a number of times and performed in mouth organ contests and stage plays. Returning to America, he became a well-known actor in numerous silent films from 1917. He died in Hollywood in 1937.

THE 1913 COBBER MOUTH ORGAN LIMERICKS

AN UNFAIR HIGHWAYMAN
There once was a knight of the road
Who a fondness for melody showed
This impudent robber rode off with a "Cobber"
He found in a wayside abode.
(Moral — Keep your eyes on your "Cobber" mouth organ.)

A WARNING
When buying mouth organs beware
If a salesman should ever declare
"It's as good as a "Cobber"
Just call him a robber —
And ask for a "Cobber" elsewhere.

TRUE
You supply the mouth
The "Cobber" does the rest
Of all mouth organs in the world
The "Cobber" is the best.

Jackson and McDonald

THE MONARCH OF MOUTH ORGANY
There was a young man of Rose Bay,
When on a mouth organ would play
'Twas a heavenly "Cobber",
A busker two bobber
The King of mouth organs they say.

HANDY AT HOPS
There was a sound of revelry by night
The boys and girls were dancing with delight
To music which they all agreed was grand
A "Cobber" mouth organ — the pocket band.

MARTIAL MUSIC
There was a young Coogee cadet,
Who said, "I like drilling, you bet
When on "Cobbers" we play,
We can march all the day,
Without getting into a perspiration.
(You think nothing of distance, when marching to a "Cobber" mouth organ band.)

COOK'S COMPLIMENT
I am a fryer of onions grey
And when I've done cooking I like to play
A "Cobber" mouth organ, the best on earth
A shilling it's price, but a pound it's worth.

MADE HER DANCE
There was a young girl of Coogee,
Who danced with much evident glee
When a "Cobber" she heard,
That her pa said, "My word,
That girl is a second Genee".

MODERN FOR ME
I cannot sing the old songs
I sang long years ago
But hear me play the songs of the day
On a two bob "Cobber" m.o.

A FAMOUS MOUTH ORGANIST
There was a young man of Newtown,
Who's name was Adolphus Fitz-Brown
The sweet music made
With the "Cobber" he played
Had won him undying renown.

EVERYBODY'S DOING IT
Everybody's doing it, doing it, doing it
Everybody's doing it, doing it, doing it
Watch that glad time couple over there
Playing on "Cobber" mouth organs so rare
What sweet music, honey I declare
It's an air, it's an air, it's an air
Ain't that music touching your heart
See the players don't they look smart
Cob, Cob, Cob, Cob, "Cobbers" start
Everybody's doing it now.

BUSINESS MAGNETS

Hickory dickory dock — the house that keeps a stock
of "Cobbers" is assured of biz,
Hickory dickory dock.
(Nothing like "Cobber" mouth organs for drawing custom.)

REALLY RIDICULOUS

Old Mother Hubbard went to the cupboard
To get her dog something to eat,
There came a big spider and sat down beside her
And played on a "Cobber" a treat.
(The idea; As if a spider could play a "Cobber" mouth organ.)

SENSIBLE SKIPPER

It was the schooner "Hesperus"
That sailed the seven seas,
And the skipper had taken his "Cobber" m.o.
To bear him company.

PUSSY'S PRAISE

Pussycat, pussycat where have you been?
I've been to Sydney and there I have seen,
"Cobber" mouth organs as sweet as a peach,
One shilling, two shillings, three shillings each.

THE FOLLY OF PETER

Peter Piper picked a peck of pickled pepper-corns
A silly thing for anyone to do;
When leisure comes our way, far better we should say
To, on a "Cobber" play a tune or two.

LAMENTABLE IGNORANCE

There was an old woman who lived in a shoe,
She had so many children she didn't know what to do.
*(Which may be accepted as incontrovertible evidence
that her education had been sadly neglected. Every
well informed mother of a large family knows that the
best thing to do is to provide the children with
"Cobber" mouth organs)*

HOW THEY CANNOT BEAT THE FAVOURITE

(A pardonable parody of a popular poem)

"Maria" said Stephen, "I'll back it, yes even
A hundred to one on any "Cobber" I'll lay
'Tis the favourite mouth organ sold in the south
And no one can beat it, attempt it who may."
(Quite enough thank you? — Ed.)

REID'S RETURN

Prime pitcher of good after dinner tales
Who's ready wit on no occasion fails
With merry serenade on a "Cobber" sweetly played
We welcome thee to sunny N.S.W.
(A popular pair — Sir George and "Cobber" mouth organs.)

THE ANCHOR'S WEIGHED

(Sydney suburban edition)

The tear fell gently from her eye
When last we parted from the gate
She was afraid I would not buy
The mouth organ that's up to date
"Weep not, fair wife" I trembling, cried
"Doubt not that I shall bring tonight
A "Cobber" for my youthful bride
To cheer her when I am out of sight".
"Dear Claude" she cried, "And must thou haste away?
My heart will break, one little moment stay".
"The tram won't wait, The tram won't wait
Farewell, farewell, have chops for tea".
(He didn't forget to buy the mouth organ.)

28 BOOMERANGS AND CRACKAJACKS

A DELIGHTFUL DREAM

I dreamt I dwelt in marble halls
With servants my words to obey,
But I also dreamt, which pleased me most
That I had a "Cobber" to play.
(In cottage or castle, the "Cobber" mouth organ is equally welcome.)

WHEN OTHER LIPS

When other lips, in other parts
On mouth organs excel,
With music which delights the hearts
Of those who near them dwell,
There may perchance at such an hour
This wise reflection be,
'None but a "Cobber" has the power
To make such melody!

THE SALVE OF LIFE

Tell me not in mournful numbers
Life is but an empty dream
For what can induce sweet slumbers,
Like a "Cobber's" notes supreme.
(As soothing as a mother's lullaby, are the dulcet tones of a "Cobber" mouth organ.)

SOUND ADVICE

The dew was falling fast,
The stars began to blink
I heard a voice it said,
"Think, pretty creature, think
The "Cobber" is the best
Mouth organ you can try,
Go put it to the test
A shilling "Cobber", buy.

STOLEN KISS

'Tis said stolen kisses are sweetest
Which may be, or may not be true,
But the melody made by a "Cobber" well played
Is the sweetest of music we know.
(On sale throughout the Cobberwealth — no, commonwealth.)

A BIG HIT

A highly successful concert was held last Thursday night at Newtown, when a number of well known artists assisted.
The hit of the evening was made by Mr A. Bawler, with that charming song — "Waiting For The Cobber Of Life", which so beautifully relates the story of a boy who has been promised a "Cobber" mouth organ on his birthday.

WEEKEND CAMPS

Young man; No matter whether you belong to the Yarra Pirates, the Bronte Brigands, the Bam Bam Swashbucklers, or any similar band of surf and sun worshippers, remember there is only one thing as indispensable as either the billy or the tin opener viz. a "Cobber" mouth organ. Verb Sap.

CROWDED BOAT RUN DOWN

It is nothing unusual to see a crowded boat run down to Manly, on Saturday afternoon, nor is it an uncommon thing to hear some of the passengers making the trip more pleasant for everybody on board, by rendering choice selections on "Cobber" mouth organs.

MYSTERIOUS DISAPPEARANCE

A young man, about seventy three years of age, has been missing from his home at North Sydney since Tuesday next. He has a very tall complexion and always moves his legs when he walks. He was last seen strolling across the harbour in a wheelbarrow, and playing melodies on a "Cobber" mouth organ.

SHE SAW A GHOST

Most people nowadays laugh at the idea of ghosts, but a lady living at Paddington has lately had an experience she is not likely to ever forget. But perhaps we had better postpone the ghost story, and devote the space at our disposal, to the brief eulogy of the "Cobber" mouth organ, the best in the world.

SHOCKING DISCOVERY

Yesterday afternoon, shortly after a party had arrived at a picnic ground, it was discovered that nobody had brought a "Cobber" mouth organ, and a picnic without a "Cobber" mouth organ is like an egg without salt, or as the Spanish girl said, a kiss without a moustache. The party returned to town, greatly depressed.

HENRY V
(Weekend version)

Once more onto the beach dear friends, once more
To weekend camps with tucker, tent and towel
And not forgetting that chief joy of life —
A "Cobber" mouth organ, the best on earth.

POOR BOY

A ship without a rudder
Would be of little worth,
A boy without a "Cobber"
Is the saddest boy on earth.

WHY BE DULL?

There was young schoolboy named Morgan
A very dull scholar, they say,
Till he purchased a "Cobber" mouth organ
Which drove all his dullness away.

A BOSKER BIRTHDAY PRESENT

"Is it your birthday, Willie dear?"
The doting dad exclaimed,
"You're ten today, my son, come here
Here's something good and famed."
(Then the proud parent extracted a "Cobber" mouth organ from the left hand pocket of his waistcoat trousers, and presented it to his son and heir.)

FATHER WILLIAM
(Modern version)

"You are old, Father William," the young man cried,
"The few locks that are left you are grey
But you're hale Father William" the young man cried,
Now what is the reason I pray?"
"Since the days of my youth" Father William replied,
"I dreaded becoming a morgue-un
So I kept myself well with a musical spell
Each day on a "Cobber" mouth organ.

PREVARICATION
A Dramatic Episode in One Act

(Scene. A Sydney music shop. Enter, a gentleman)
GENTLEMAN: "I want a Cobber mouth organ, please."
SALESMAN: "Mouth organ, sir? Yes sir, certainly."
(produces some alleged mouth organs)
"Here you are, sir."
GENTLEMAN: "But I asked for a Cobber mouth organ."
SALESMAN: "Yes sir, but we don't stock the Cobber. These are just as good."
GENTLEMAN: (Severely) "Young man, you have missed your vocation; you should have been an advance agent for a travelling circus."
(Exit indignantly to find an up to date music shop.)

AN HEIR BY AIRS

There was a young man from Taree
A "Cobber" mouth organist he,
So sweetly he played,
That a wealthy old maid
Bequeathed him a great property.

"A 'COBBERY' COROBBOREE"

There was a young man of Casino,
Who, when he went out on a beano
Would play a solo
On a "Cobber" m.o.
And land home at night, all seren-o.
(A musical mate to keep you straight, is a "Cobber" mouth organ.)

DOTTY BY DISAPPOINTMENT

Now here is a horrible tale
Of a musical man of Moss Vale
In a shop he went mad,
On hearing they had
No "Cobber" mouth organs for sale.

A BOSKER BILLET

There was a young waiter at Mittagong,
Whose duties were pleasant and light
In the daytime he just had to hit a gong,
And play on a "Cobber" at night.

QUITE EXCUSABLE

There was an old lady of Harden,
Who sat all day long in her garden
And played "Sweet And Low"
On a "Cobber" m.o.
A fad we can readily pardon.
(For young and old, there is nothing more soothing than the dulcet strains of a "Cobber" mouth organ.)

HOW TO HOOK 'EM

There was a young lady named May
Who on a mouth organ could play
'Twas a "Cobber", ye ken,
So she charmed all the men
And married a squatter from Hay.

30 BOOMERANGS AND CRACKAJACKS

Australian brand-name mouth organs c.1913
The Rozella by A.P. Sykes of Melbourne

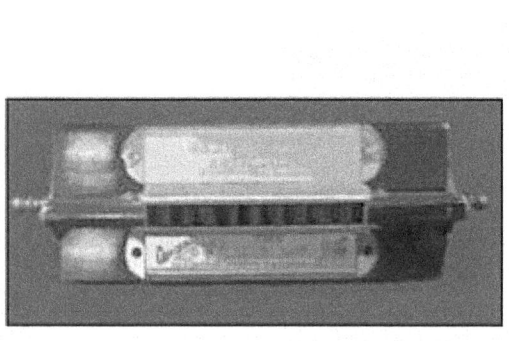

Four-sided Wallaroo   *J. Albert & Son Kangaroo with box, Wallaroo and Coo-ee*

In outback Australia 1900s –
a stockman plays a mouth organ solo

Chapter Three

Off to War and Into School

By the end of the Boer War, the authorities at the Langwarrin Army Training Camp in Victoria had recognised the value of the mouth organ as a morale booster for the troops still in training. In 1904, a Mouth Harmonica Contest was organised and eventually won by the Senior Cadets Team and D Company, with the 6th Australian Infantry Regiment coming a close second. Government members awarded trophies to the winning teams and the "Adelaide Advertiser", 4th April commented:

'The mouth organ as a military adjunct seems capable of great developments. Many of the companies on their return yesterday from a long route march, formed their musical men up in the centre of the companies, and in the absence of a band these led the men singing and enlivened the march, with the result that a speedy and pleasant return from a hard day's duty was secured.'

Eion S. Campbell (right), in the Boer War. (Campbell later became the Australian Mouth Organ Champion of 1940)

D Company, 6th A.I.R. at Langwarrin Army Camp in 1904

The Lonely Soldiers' Guild, a London-based organisation to help World War I Australian troops serving in Egypt at that time, sent out a newspaper plea in 1915:

"We appeal for gifts of gramophones and other musical instruments to relieve the tedium of the lonely soldier. Banjos, mouth organs, anything that would disperse the weighty silence of weightier dullness in the long monotonous evenings, spent either in camp or on-board ship".

In May of that year, the Australian Light Horse Brigade departed Egypt to join the battle which was raging at Gallipoli. "The Argus" reported they were telling jokes and laughing and singing as they marched through the city of Heliopolis that night, while mouth organs kept up an accompaniment. As the tragedy of Gallipoli and other battlefields unfolded, hundreds upon hundreds of wounded Australian troops were sent home in hospital trains.

On one such trainload leaving Cairo in 1916, those who were able, made their way into carriages, settled down for the journey home, pulled out their mouth organs and 'played some familiar airs'.

32 BOOMERANGS AND CRACKAJACKS

*Upgraded models of the Scorcher:
Popular in Australia until c.1920*

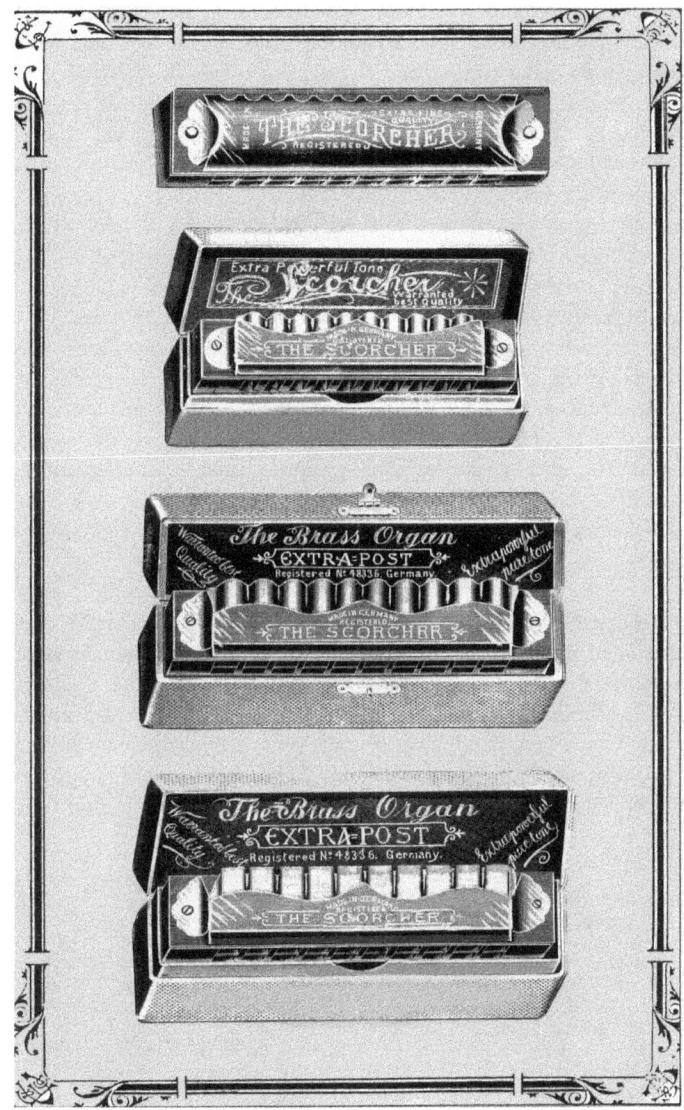

Benefits, processions and organised gatherings were held regularly to aid the war-wounded. A spectacular event in Melbourne on 4th September 1915 by The Sick and Wounded Soldiers Fund included an Amy Castles concert and a street procession in which about fifty wounded Gallipoli heroes marched, culminating in a huge fair which contained entertainments of all kinds. While a biograph picture was screened, the forty-piece Crackajack Band performed. "The Argus" of Monday 6th September, described the outfit as 'delightful' and proclaimed: *'The volume of sound which came from the mouth organs was surprising'.*

Appeals for mouth organs by organisations such as the Lonely Soldiers' Guild brought an overwhelming response from Australians, resulting in the instrument giving comfort to many diggers throughout the ordeals of the Great War.

Commenting on the response of donated mouth organs, "The Argus" said:

'Hundreds of these instruments have been received from kindly donors and the result can be heard on all sides. Not only do cheerful sounds emit from billets and dug-outs, but many of the detachments and small bodies of men moving from one point to another now march to the sentimental notes of "Tipperary" or the hit of "Get Out and Get Under", instead of tramping the slush in silence'.

The paper went on to say that even small children had made donations of their 'cherished possessions' and quoted a note that was sent by a small boy to one of their collection centres:

"Dear Sir' Allison and me are sending our mouth organs for the soldiers. They aren't new ones but I hadn't any sixpences.

With Love…"

Of all the many charitable gatherings and concerts for the war effort held all over Australia, there is one that is of particular interest regarding the mouth organ. It took place on the Saturday afternoon of 21st August 1915. Held at the Melbourne Cricket Ground and advertised as The Children's Great Patriotic Day, it announced the appearance of the Victorian Patriotic Crackajack Band. One of the event organisers, a Mr S. E. Hambleton of Collingwood, had sent out a call for one hundred and three mouth organ players (boys only), to make up the band. The sound of over one hundred Crackajack mouth organs echoing around the MCG must have been impressive.

Right: An Anzac Service at the Melbourne Cricket Ground in 1917

Australian children certainly made a worthy musical contribution to the War Effort, but also got themselves into all sorts of trouble with their mouth organs in other ways, judging by the following examples:

Well before the War, on a hot tropical night in Queensland in January 1897, two young boys were sitting on the Queen's Wharf in Bundaberg, smoking and listening to their friend, Sam Schofield playing the mouth organ.

"The Brisbane Courier" explained that Sam was sitting on an empty rum-cask and unfortunately dropped a lighted match into the cask cork-hole. The result was an explosion that not only interrupted Sam's performance, but also blew him, his mouth organ and the rum-cask lid into the Burnett River. It was certainly an impressive musical grand finale and you might have thought that it was the last anyone would ever hear of Sam and his mouth organ. This was not the case however, because he was out of the river and on his way home in no time, suffering only a few minor injuries.

Hedley Martin, a twelve-year-old mouth organ player of Launceston in Tasmania, had an adventure of a different kind many years later, in June of 1921. "The Argus" explained that Hedley was a newspaper-boy who plied his trade daily on the Launceston Wharf and the steamer-boat, while awaiting its departure to Melbourne. He was on the "Nairana" steamer and was a bit slow in getting some change for a customer when it left the wharf and headed off down the Tamar River, before he could get off. Hedley's first instinct was to sit down and have a good cry, then inform one of the ship's officers of his predicament. He was given blankets and a meal to see him through the night's journey across the Bass Straight and into Port Phillip Bay Melbourne, where the police who had been informed of his plight took him to their headquarters. The sights and sounds of the big smoke set off a spark of some sort in Hedley and he loudly proclaimed that he did not want to return to Launceston. Telling the police he loved the Melbourne trams, he informed them that he had not before realised that 'Melbourne was so big' and 'Tassie so slow'.

His enthusiasm grew and in no time he had taken out his mouth organ and was giving selections of Scottish songs and popular airs to the passing Melbourne shoppers and pedestrians, soon attracting a large crowd that donated an amount of pocket-money. Hedley had been quick to make the most of a bad situation but his dreams of becoming a mouth organ star on Australia's mainland came to an end when the police put him back on the "Nairana" and sent him home to Launceston, still carrying his bundle of yesterday's papers and his mouth organ.

Above: "The Duet": A 1913 portrait

Above: On a Melbourne beach C.1913

"BONZER" MOUTH ORGANS

The Powerful Tone of the
Bonzer Mouth Organ
is Simply Grand

Made in Several sizes.
Prices 2/6d., 3/-, 3/6d., 4/-

Sole Agents: ALLAN'S
Melbourne, Bendigo, Ballarat, Geelong, Adelaide

Above: The Bonzer sold briefly by Allan & Co. in the 1920s. Bonzer accordions were also available

Magpie Mouth Organs

Every "Magpie" model represents exceptional value.
Best metal reeds produce most delightful tone.
European make 2/6, 3/6, 5/-

The Magpie was marketed from 1913 until the mid 1920s by Macrows of Melbourne

'Never work with children or animals' is a well-known rule of many performers. Mouth organ soloist, Mr D. Butler of Darwin was one of a number of musicians and bands at the monthly Unemployed Camp Dance in Darwin in July 1931 and was eager to impress the crowd with his playing. It was reported in the "Northern Territory Times" that when his turn came, a little 'tiny-tot' completely stole his thunder.

This regular benefit or charity concert was a popular event in Darwin and always featured a large range of musical acts and performers, on this occasion consisting of The Manilla String Band and The Thursday Island String Band, with violin solos by Mr A. Boath and a dancer, Mr B. Domasco.

An unexpected and unrehearsed item occurred during the rendering of a mouth organ solo by Mr. D. Butler, when a tiny, three-year-old laddie danced gaily onto the floor and kept time to the music in a solo dance. He was quite happy, flitting around the room and was quite oblivious to all save the lilting strains of the mouth organ, but he footed it so neatly, that at the end of the solo, an encore was eagerly demanded by the delighted lookers-on'.

NSW State Mouth Organ Champion James Sinclair gives a Boomerang Mouth Organ Demonstration to Cootamundra Public School students in 1927

In the mid 1930s three members of the Melbourne Boys Club Mouth Organ Band display three different 'grips' as they prepare for a contest

The renowned Australian composer and musician, Alfred Hill, spent much of his life in New Zealand and gained a strong interest and passion in Maori music and culture, often weaving such themes into his compositions.

His endeavours also gave Australians a cultural and educational insight into Maori traditions and music through his concerts, in which he featured visiting performers and bands in the 1920s and 1930s.

One such group The Tahiwis, already famous in New Zealand, recorded over twenty sides in Sydney at the Columbia studios, when they arrived in 1930. They were released on the Parlophone label in Australia and New Zealand (and have since been reissued).

One track in particular, "He Puru Taitama", written by Kingi Tahiwi a brother of the group members, became one of the best-known Maori songs ever recorded.

The Tahiwis

Henare Tahiwi

The Tahiwis of Otaki, were a vocal and multi-instrumental band, comprising Henare and his sisters, Hinehou and Weno. Henare (1885-1955), plays mouth organ on some of the many vocal tracks and one impressive instrumental mouth organ solo track is included and titled: "A Poi Dance". The Rhythmic Three are credited as the accompanists: the first mouth organ recording in Australia by an overseas artist.

Alfred Hill arranged some of the Tahiwi recordings and still showed a fondness for the instrument five years later, when he judged the 1935 National Championships for J. Albert & Son, stating that he considered the mouth organ to be 'Australia's national instrument'.

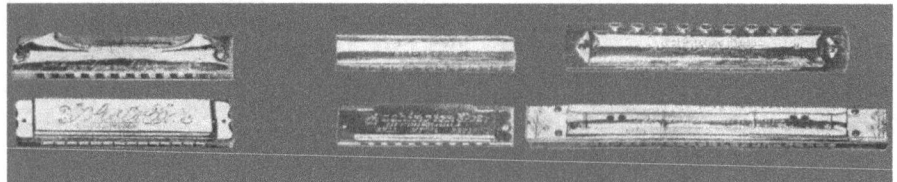
Empire Band and Astra from Czechoslovakia- Piff Paff, Tip Top, Washington Post, Regimental Band from Germany. On sale in Australia in the 1920s

Chapter Four

Champions, Kings and Professors

A number of mouth organ contests were held in Australia up to the end of the nineteenth-century, most being of local or amateur variety.

The first Australian Championship in 1899 organised by J. Albert & Son and held in Sydney at the Golden Gate Club was a cut-above these. The Golden Gate was an old boxing and athletics hall behind a shop-front facade in George Street, their motto being 'boxing shows may come and go, but we go on forever'. They often held amateur boxing nights which usually resulted in a free-for-all that had rowdy audiences howling with laughter, so a mouth organ contest or in this case a National Championship, won by Walter Omond, was a good idea for some light entertainment before the serious boxing bouts of the night got under way.

Boxing underway at the Golden Gate 1898   *The Club as a shooting gallery in 1909*

George Hunt who originally took up the challenge but later withdrew for reasons unknown, took part successfully in another two-man event in Brisbane at the Theatre Royal in 1910 against vaudeville performer, Tom Hedley winning five pounds and a gold medal, presented by the theatre manager, Ted Holland. Hedley was a multi-instrumentalist and comedian who played mouth organ, xylophones, one-string violin, cow-bells and rows of bottles, dressed as a tramp and was known as the 'Musical Moke', an act that seems to have been inspired by American, Will Van Allen, 'The Musical Tramp', who had toured Australia and promoted the Crackajack in 1904.

Famous Australian stage performer, Harry Sadler began his career as 'The Mouth Organ King' around 1900 and as with so many other vaudeville artists, the mouth organ remained an important part of his act as a comedian and song and dance man. He performed for around twenty years, and became a successful entrepreneur as well, managing theatres and touring vaudeville shows throughout Australia, including the promotion of overseas acts. He was sued by singer, Phyllis Faye in Perth on a charge of slander against herself and a fellow-performer, Arthur Morley. Suffering ill-health, he committed suicide by jumping from a railway bridge in Leichhardt, Sydney in 1919.

40 BOOMERANGS AND CRACKAJACKS

Howard's Music Warehouse in George St. Sydney (see shops on the left in photo), stocked a large range of mouth organs.
On the evening of the 8th. of August 1894, they held a mouth organ contest at their premises. On the next day, an anonymous but very detailed review of the event was published in the "Evening News" and is reproduced on the following page.

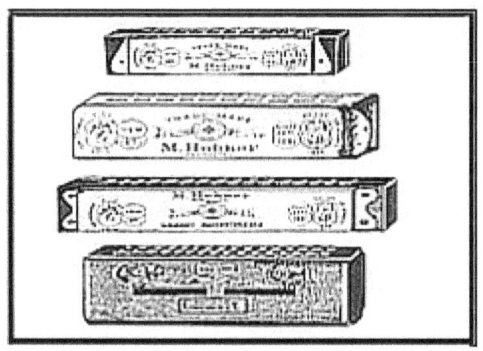

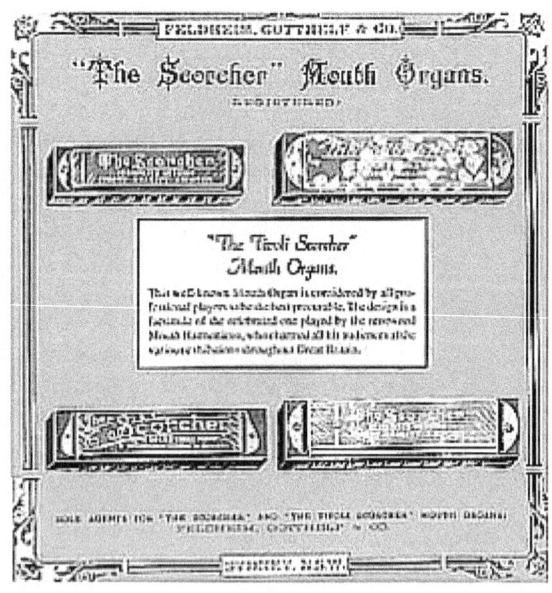

The Lyrical Larrikin
A Review of Howard's Music Warehouse Mouth Organ Contest : Sydney 1894

After having decided either to go and hear the Premier propound his policy at the Protestant Hall last night or to see his rival "Mr. Harry Foran, gentleman" egged and floured outside, we altered our mind and decided to go and hear another kind of 'mouth organ contest' which we saw advertised in the Evening News.

The Scene of the contest was Howard's Music Warehouse on Brickfield Hill and thither we went much marvelling what manner of instrument a 'mouth organ' could be and the sort of music it would be likely to afford. Enquiry elicited that 'this organ was a harp' and that this harp no more resembled a harp than it did Mons. Wiegand's superb pet at the Centennial Hall, or the infernal Italian barrell organ.

It proved to be nothing more than the simple little reed instrument into which the lyrical larrikin pours all the sentiment of his soul when wooing his ladylove either at Chowder or Bondi.

The technical term for the instrument is 'concert harp' and it has of late become commoner in Sydney than the penny whistle or the concertina. The organiser of the contest, who surely must be a lineal descendant of 'Howard the Philanthropist', pointed out that it was the first of a series arranged, not so much to promote the sale of mouth organs among the musically illiterate male and female youth as to elevate their sentiments, refine their manners and to make them worthy in every sense to hold a golden harp in the celestial choir where the moralising influences of the terrestrial mouth organ are neither known or required.

He frankly admitted that he got his 'scheme of musical redemption' from no less a personage than Mr. Wm. McMillan, who had once publicly declared that music alone could charm the larrikin out of the land. Pointing to a group of youths who were present, the promoter enthusiastically referred to them as some of the most 'remarkable manipulators of the mouth organ' he had ever heard and promised that their performance would astonish us. And so it did

Apparently these contest are conducted on the 'Carrington Handicap Principle' being run off or rather blown off in heats or batches. The contest is judged by points in 'effects, tempo, tone and vamping' by a duly appointed adjudicator, who on this occasion proved to be none other than Mr. G.D. Simon who acted as sole adjudicator at the last Wallsend Eisteddfod.

The competitors drew lots as to the order in which they should compete, and that question once decided, they went to work with a will. There was no conductor or accompanist, each performer being all in all to himself, even to composing his own selections, as was the case in one instance. Each competitor chose his own selections of which he played two.

These for the most part consisted of popular melodies or dance music, such as delighteth those whose souls find vent through a mouth organ, among them being "E Dunno Where E Are", "Swanee River", "Bluebells of Scotland", "Champagne Charlie", "Knocked 'Em in the Old Kent Road", the "Emigrant's Farewell", "Nancy Lee" and the "Chowder Bay Waltz", the last-named being a composition of the performer himself, a youth of some 17 or 18 years of age.

It is due to the composer to say that "Chowder Bay" sounded no better nor worse than "Blue Danube" when played on the mouth organ.

Whether the performers are elevated and refined in the manner indicated by Mr. McMillan is a matter of opinion. Certain it is however, that the mouth organ is fast becoming the instrument of the people. Its cheapness and simplicity give music to those who neither have nor desire any other and if, in the language of the promoter of last night's unique contest - "the mouth organ is a moral agent, it makes the young men who play it at random by ear feel some sort of a love for the beautiful which is in every human heart, because if they did not feel at heart they could not play as sweetly by ear" - then the mouth organ with all its comical concomitants must not be accounted a nuisance.

Various kinds of attachments or 'improvements' as they were sometimes called, became available and some of these were on-sale in Australia. (See p. 95 for a few examples). They sometimes took the mouth organ into very different catagories of 'musical instruments' such as the Harp-o-Chord of 1902, a combination harpsichord and mouth organ and a few years later in 1906, newspapers announced a new instrument by an American inventor from New Jersey. The illustration from the time, showed a handle-held box with a mouth organ attached and paper rolls inside. You could get a tune by turning the handle as you played, a similar process to the music rolls in player pianos. A much improved version of this came to Australia from the U.S., much later in 1928 as the Rolmonica. Walter Omond, the 1899 Australian Mouth Organ Champion, submitted his invention for a mouth organ 'improvement' in 1904. It was described as 'a sliding mouth-piece and triller' and it seems that nothing more was heard of it , although a very similar apparatus appeared in 1937, a few years after Omond's death. It was called the Glaz-o-Phone. (see p. 101).

Sydney Dickens invented an 'attachment' for mouth organs in 1908. Born in 1884, he arrived in Australia in 1887 with his family from England and they eventually settled in Carlton, Melbourne. He worked as a night-watchman which resulted in him being shot in the leg by an intruder, while on-guard at a factory premises one night, after which he found work as a tailor's presser, a job also held by Omond alongside his vaudeville engagements around Melbourne. Dickens called his invention the Echophone. It was an oval-shaped two-piece horn which could be bolted on to a mouth organ and adjusted inwards or outward by a sliding mechanism for different volume levels. It also came in various sizes. It was manufactured and sold in Australia throughout 1908 and 1909 in music shops and was also available from Dickens himself. Around this time, cylinder records titled "Mouth Organ Medley" Parts One and Two by a Professor Dickens were released on the obscure Melbourne Empire label. Research by the Author suggested that Charles Dickens impersonator and highly regarded actor, Clement May recorded these tracks, with later information also coming to hand by a descendant, that May's wife, Florence could have also had some involvement. She was an expert mouth organist who sometimes stood in as a 'behind-the-scenes player' for stage plays such as "Struck Oil". The discovery of a patent application in England, for the Sydney Dickens Echophone by British Harmonica player and researcher, Pat Missin points more directly to Dickens himself as the 'Professor', possibly even using the Echophone on the recordings. Throughout 1925, both May and Dickens were often featured in separate regular spots on Melbourne radio 3LO with their respective Charles Dickens recitals and mouth organ segments. Dickens also became a member of the "Childrens Hour". They both then attended the National Mouth Organ Championship in Ballarat, where Dickens competed and received an Honorable Mention for his performance.

CHAMPIONS, KINGS AND PROFESSORS 43

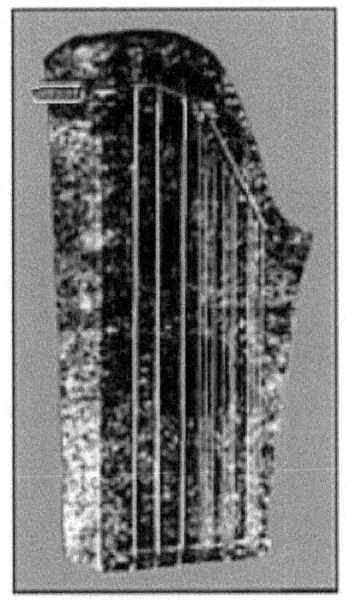

1906 American invention
1902 Harp-o-Chord

Sydney Dickens (1884-1965)

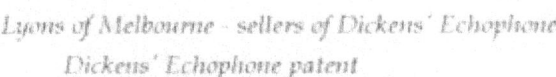

Lyons of Melbourne - sellers of Dickens' Echophone
Dickens' Echophone patent

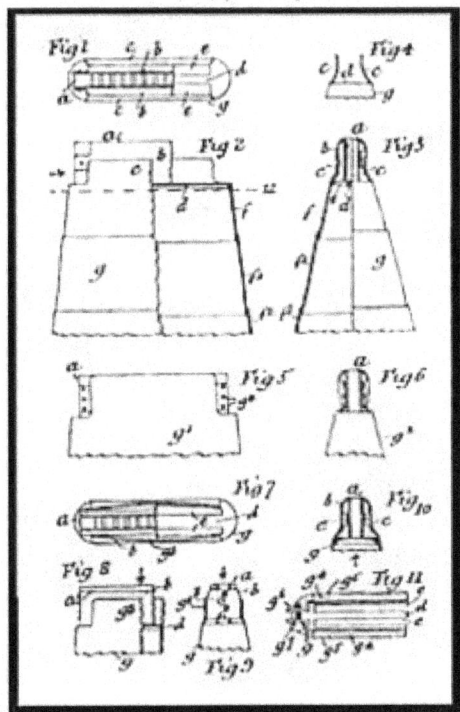

TO Mouth Organ Players.—Dickens's Patent Mouth Organ, Echophone, must wonderful musical instrument. Country stores should stock them.

DICKENS'S Echophone increases the volume of sound, equal to 3 mouth organs, greatly improves the tone.

DICKENS'S Echophones, unsurpassed for picnics, socials, concerts, at homes; ladies, get one, easily played, will surprise you.

DICKENS'S Patent Echophone, suitable for rich or poor, anyone can play it; country residents note this.

DICKENS'S Echophone, a wonderful attachment for the mouth organ, patented Great Britain, Commonwealth and New Zealand.

DICKENS'S Echophone, at Meinhardt's, Gertrude-st., Lyons, Bourke-st., and S. Dickens, patentee, 'A' Drummond-st., Carlton.

DICKENS'S Echophone, from 1/9 to 5/6; procurable at Lyons' New Music Shop, Bourke-st. Last a lifetime.

DICKENS'S patent Echophone.—Miners, Bushmen, Sailors, Firemen, Men o' Wargmen, buy one; will be greatly delighted.

44 BOOMERANGS AND CRACKAJACKS

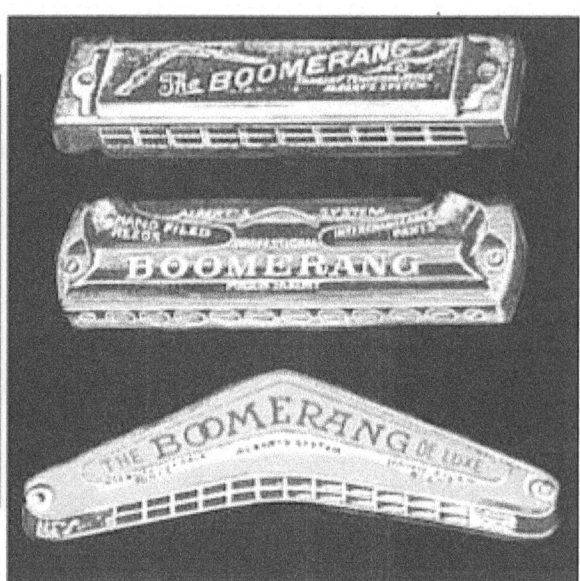

The up-dated J. Albert & Son Boomerang range from 1924:
Tiny, Tiny De Luxe and Pocket
Miniature, Miniature Professional and Miniature De Luxe
large, Professional and De Luxe

Joe Aronson and his Orchestra play Boomerang De Luxe mouth organs at the Sydney Trocadero in 1927

CHAMPIONS, KINGS AND PROFESSORS   45

J. Albert & Son mouth organs for Australia and New Zealand

Below: For special promotions the Tiny De Luxe was sold as the Baby De Luxe and the Tiny became the Little Boomerang

THE BABY BOOMERANG.

Visitors to the show should see the remarkable novelty being demonstrated in the flower section, and will be amazed at the manner in which the little Boomerang when fired from the shooting apparatus flies into the air, and spins right back to the hand. It is perfectly genuine, and anybody can fire it. A remarkably free gift is being made in connection with this novelty. With each one sold is presented the compliments of J. Albert and Sons, music publishers, Sydney, and a genuine baby boomerang mouth organ.

After his 1925 Australian Championship win, P.C. Spouse signed a recording contract with Columbia studios in Sydney making ten 78 rpm recordings between 1926 and 1936, five of which were top-sellers.

He won the 1927, 1928 and 1935 National Championships as well as numerous state and local events and promoted the Boomerang for J. Albert & Son for around twenty five years, playing regularly at concerts and picture theatre interval spots. As part of his novelty act Spouse would also create music from wood axes, fire shovels, household guttering and funnels, match boxes and books.

After his final recording contract had expired in 1937, 'P.C. Spouse Mouth Organs' became available through Mick Simmons Ltd of Sydney and Newcastle NSW, with the engraving :
'used by P.C. Spouse' on the cover-plates of F.A. Bohm World's Fame mouth organs.
A project that would not have been to acceptable to J. Albert & Son, they were off the market by year's end.

J. Albert & Son reminder that you're never too young or old to play a Boomerang mouth organ

Van used by Spouse in his role as a travelling shoe-sales representative in the 1930s

One night in September 1928, after a performance at the National Theatre in Braidwood NSW, Spouse was heading for the coast over Clyde Mountain on the Kings Highway, when bumps in the unsealed dirt road caused items to bounce from his car. While walking back to retrieve them, the handbrake slipped and the car rolled off the road and over a 60 metre cliff. After managing to find and save some valuables, Spouse told the press that all was lost and that the car had been 'smashed to smithereens'.

CHAMPIONS, KINGS AND PROFESSORS 47

The Coliseum at Ballarat

After this event mouth organ contests by the hundreds took place throughout the country, eventually including mouth organ band and women's and children's solo categories. Gold, Silver and Bronze medals along with cups and trophies were fiercely sought after. By the end of the decade the instrument was being taught in schools.

This activity would continue for fifteen years until World War II demanded more young players for the battlefront and the mouth organ was off to war again.

Never far behind J. Albert & Son and the Boomerang, was Allan & Co. of Melbourne with their rival brand, the Crackajack. Soon after the new Boomerangs were released, Allan & Co. introduced their upgraded models. All models were given newer style cover-plates and brand new models were also introduced over the following decade. Allan & Co. began to compete strongly with J. Albert & Son, becoming equally involved in competitions and band formations as well. By this time the German Hohner Company, now the world's largest, had decided they needed a more direct sales position in Australia and so they opened an official agency in Melbourne in 1936. Kurt Jacob was sent out from Germany to open up the business and become involved in the local harmonica scene.

The 1926 Championship at the Coliseum. The winner, Stan Andrews stands centre, third row back

48 BOOMERANGS AND CRACKAJACKS

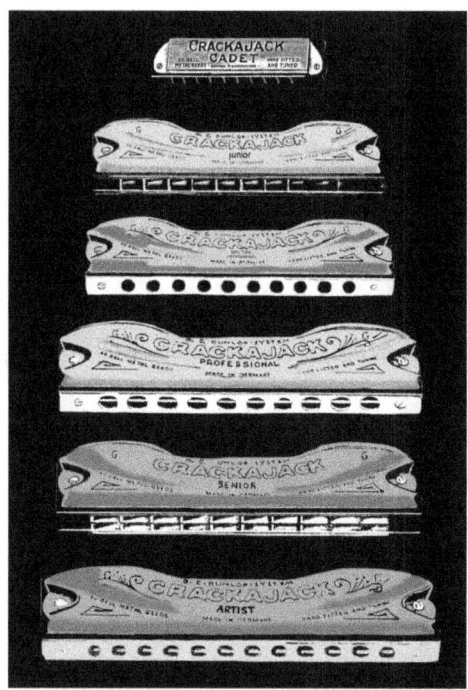

A selection of the Allan & Co. advertisements and the upgraded Crackajack range from 1927
Cadet
Junior
Miniature Professional
Professional
Senior
Artist
Miniature Concert
Concert
Concert Grand
Tremolo Concert

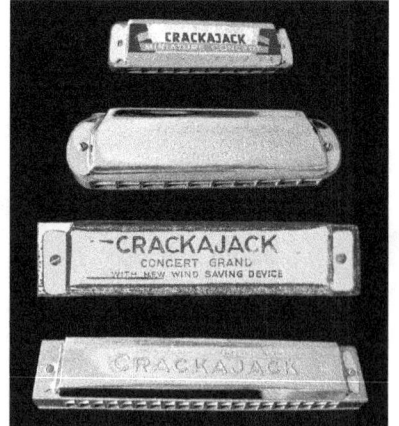

CHAMPIONS, KINGS AND PROFESSORS 49

The 3LO 1927 Australian Championship Trophy won by Harold Collier at the 3LO Radio Station studio in Melbourne

Harold Collier's Crackajack Mouth Organ Orchestra with their band wagon

Allan & Co. were not content to just stand by and watch P. C. Spouse promoting the Boomerang and soon began preparations for an alternative championship in Melbourne. First mooted as a Melbourne competition, it soon evolved into a separate 1927 Australian Championship contest, held at the same time and in direct competition to the Ballarat event. Harold Collier had competed at Ballarat but became the Crackajack exponent when he won and was soon out and about, promoting the alternative mouth organ.

But Collier did not stop there. Over the next decade he worked tirelessly in Melbourne, helping with the formation of children's and women's bands and became conductor of the award-winning Melbourne Ladies Crackajack Mouth Organ Band. He later took out first place again, this time at South Street, when he won the 1936 Solo Championship.

After a further win by Spouse in 1928, the mouth organ events were taken over by the Ballarat South Street Committee, which was eventually joined by the Victorian Mouth Organ Bands Association (VMOBA). Although J. Albert & Son were now no longer involved with South Street, it was evident that Frank Albert had created a major resurgence in the mouth organ's popularity in 1925.

Aside from competitions of every category held all over Australia, South Street was experiencing unparalleled activity with unprecedented crowds at the Eisteddfod and the mouth organ events were becoming the biggest-ever draw card. An Australian Band Championship was introduced in 1929 and won by The Ballarat Harmonica Band. They made two recordings in Melbourne after their win.

The Ballarat Harmonica Band

Lillian Clark (right) and Harold Collier Success at South Street 1933

A Women's Mouth Organ Championship took place at yet another competition event at the Geelong West City Town Hall in 1931 with Edna Blyth taking out first place. Later in 1933, the newly formed VMOBA started an annual Street Marching Competition at South Street resulting in thousands of spectators cheering the bands through the streets of Ballarat, as they made their way in uniforms to the Coliseum. This event would become a full day mouth organ extravaganza. Another separate national competition from the annual South Street contests was held in 1935 at the Scots Church in the City of Sydney Eisteddfod by J. Albert & Son, which saw another win by P. C. Spouse.

A fire destroyed the Coliseum in 1936 and left the South Street Society with the problem of finding an alternative venue for that year's Eisteddfod. The old Alfred Hall was cleaned up, given a new coat of paint and made ready in time for the event. For the mouth organists, there were other changes coming as well. In the 1937 band competitions, a more extensive use of the new chromatic harmonica was noticed, brought about to a large extent by the presence of the Hohner Company's new official Australian representative, Kurt Jacob. He had arrived and set up in Melbourne in the previous year and started promoting the Hohner, particularly the advanced chromatic instrument. Hohner, always a top-seller in Australia would now be given an even larger profile. Braham Solomon, one of Hohner's leading dealers who worked with the English company, Oppenheimer, became a mentor of sorts to Jacob, helping him to get the business started. As an avid follower of the South Street Competitions, he donated an impressive award to be given to the winning band each year, called The Hohner Perpetual Shield Trophy.

Braham Solomon

The Hohner Perpetual Shield Trophy

Disagreements between South Street and the VMOBA resulted in another separate competition held in 1938. This was the Australasian Band Championship at the Plaza Theatre, Geelong and won by the Geelong West City Harmonica Band and there was further contention when Leslie Jennings made history by winning the 1939 Championship playing a chromatic harmonica. Many of the players felt this win was unfair as most had not progressed to, or had any inclination to switch from the diatonic instrument. The problem was settled in the 1940 event when the two were separated. The Championship would be diatonic only, with a separate smaller contest for the chromatic players.

The end was nigh however, with World War II claiming young players from bands all over Australia and only a handful would re-form after the hostilities had ended. The South Street Eisteddfod itself was temporarily cancelled but the Mouth Organ Championships were gone from Ballarat forever. It was fitting that the winner of the final event in 1940 was Eion S. Campbell, Queensland recording artist and radio personality. Campbell had served in the Boer War and World War I and after his national win was off to war again, this time as a correspondent for the "Whizz Bang" magazine.

52 BOOMERANGS AND CRACKAJACKS

Sydney Dickens (second left) with Little Miss Kookaburra and wireless station 3LO Children's Hour program crew in Melbourne 1925

Above - from Left:

Fire destroys the Coliseum in Ballarat in 1936
Geelong West City Town Hall
Replacement venue for the Competitions - the Alfred Hall
Alfred Hall interior
Plaza Theatre Geelong on the left

The mouth organ became well established in Australian wireless programming throughout 1925 after the first performances by the Errol Street State School Crackajack Band and Sydney Dickens. Heard in solo, duet and band form, items in Sydney by Mr A. W. Forrest in June were followed throughout 1926 on Melbourne's 3LO by James Mayger, Waldo Burgoyne and T. J. Mitchell with his sons, James and John. Australian Champion P. C. Spouse then began regular performances on Sydney's 2FC.

By the mid 1930s so much had changed. Men's, women's and children's bands were playing all over the country, both live and on the radio, championships were being held, recordings sold. A new development was the emergence of the chromatic harmonica.
Some of 'the older folk' were starting to reminisce about their early experiences with the instrument and the fond memories they held of their threepenny mouth organs.
Alec H. Chisholm touched on this when he wrote a short article for the children's section of "The Argus" on 1st February 1934, titled 'Notes for Boys'.

'Reading a few days ago, of a girls' mouth-organ band appearing in public, I was reminded that in recent times the once humble mouth organ has gained a new dignity. In other years the playing of this little instrument was almost wholly a recreation of boys. When a girl had a turn at a mouth-organ - perhaps borrowed when her brother was not looking - she played apologetically, as if knowing she was intruding and her skill was about that of the average girl kicking a football. Nowadays however, we not only hear of numerous skilled players among girls, but we see them going to the lengths of forming bands and wearing uniforms. This is mildly alarming and I am glad to be assured that the boys are not giving in without a struggle. There are, it appears, many boys' and young mens' bands, and all are swelling their chests with enthusiasm.
Whatever be the cause of this revival, I for one am very glad that the "matey" little mouth-organ has come into its own. The only thing I regret is that some bands have dropped the familiar term in favour of "harmonica". Doubtless, a mouth-organ by any other name would sound as sweet, but "harmonica" is rather too imposing for one who never heard the term as a boy. In my school days a lad who could play a "mouthie" at all well was a subject of envy to the rest of us. We all yearned to be good players. Failing this, we chummed up with the musical lad and urged him on to extended performances. Most of his items were old favourites of the "Swanee River" variety, with perhaps a few hymns added. Others were taken from gramaphones, which then were coming into favour. Others again were acquired by listening to the local brass band. It was all a matter of playing by ear. The fact that none of us could read music did not affect our enjoyment. We had some very pleasant times with the mouth-organs in those bush days and as I have said, the mere mention of the term now revives happy memories.
But the mouth-organ was not our only boyish instrument. There was, for example, the Jew's harp. Pending a discussion on the subject, perhaps someone can tell us what has become of that quaint little device.'

(Alec H. Chisholm, born in Victoria in 1890, was an author, journalist and ornithologist and is regarded as one of Australia's first true conservationists. He was awarded an OBE and an Australian Natural History Medallion for his life-long work on the subject).

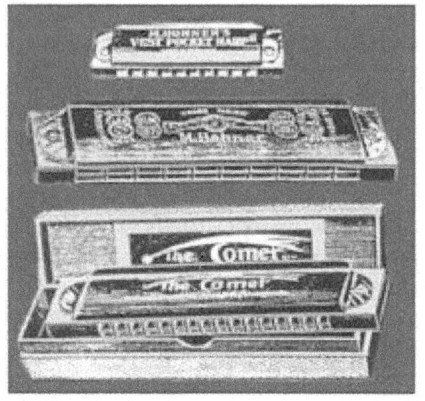

Popular Hohner models in Australia from the early 1900s

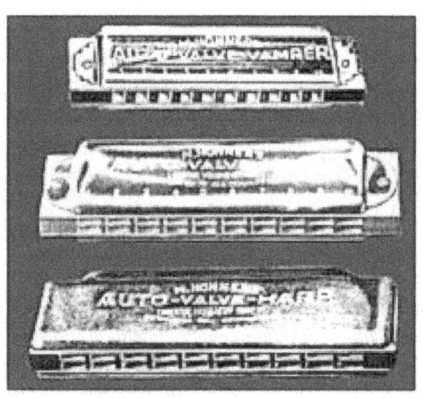

The Auto-Valve Harp, marketed by Hohner as an 'Australian' model in the 1930s, but available both overseas and in Australia from c. 1910

The Hohner Echophone – popular with vaudeville performers in the 1920s

Chapter Five

The Dark Side of the Mouth Organ

In advertisements, mouth organs were almost always described as respectable instruments for education and enjoyment, but looking through various news stories from the past can reveal a different side. As an instrument that enjoyed immense popularity with people from all different walks of life over many decades, it was only natural that it saw the seamier side of life on occasions. This was indeed the case, when it was revealed that the mouth organ played a part in offences that ranged from 'arrest for nuisance', through to outright murder.

In October 1909, George Lacey was charged with 'being an inebriate'. He was described in the "Adelaide Advertiser" as 'an old man who makes discord on a mouth organ, with a vigorous rattling of a pair of bones, in the streets opposite hotels'.

Many years later in April 1921, unfortunate George Rainey was arrested and fined for disrupting traffic in Bourke Street Melbourne. In "The Argus," Rainey was described as 'a one-man-band' dressed in 'a blue uniform with elaborate red and white facings'. He simultaneously played a mouth organ, whistle, a drum, cymbals and other instruments. The police officer had instructed him to stop playing, a request he refused which then led to his arrest.

Five other men were in Court on the same day as Rainey on charges of playing music in the streets and obstructing pedestrians and traffic. They were members of a 'returned soldier's band' and it is not known if a mouth organ player was amongst them, although it could be presumed that this almost certainly would have been the case.

Showing no mercy to the 'returned soldiers' they were all fined, with "The Argus" commenting that at last, some police action had been taken to 'check the itinerant street musician pest'.

Archibald Luhrs (or Luhers), was known to the Melbourne police as an 'idle and disorderly person' and a chronic alcoholic. Over a number of years he got into trouble around various pubs by playing his mouth organ and asking for donations which were immediately consumed at the bar. Mindful of his 'medical condition', he was sometimes pardoned by the judge on the condition that he take a pledge to 'give up the grog', but he did also serve a number of gaol sentences. At one of his appearances at the Brunswick Court in January 1928, "The Argus" reported that Luhrs told the Judge: *"I was playing the mouth organ. I led a mouth organ band in Albury. I am a professional mouth organ player and I am on my way to Geelong"*.

A part of his sentence on this occasion was an order to leave the Brunswick area immediately, but his was the last case heard at the court that day and soon after he was found still in the police courtyard, playing his mouth organ and entertaining a collection of 'constables, litigants and other persons'.

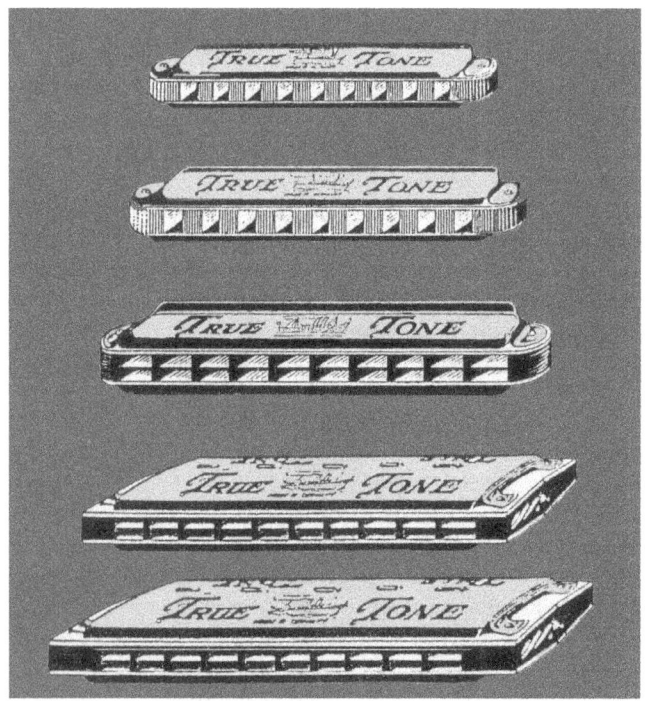

The True Tone range: available in Australia in the 1920s and 1930s

Many new mouth organs were on display in Australian shops from the early 1920s. Both the Gypsy and Army Band contained double sets of brass reeds for three shillings each and one of many novelty items, the Mandola, featured a fixed-tube apparatus that magnified the volume 'for a more pleasing tone'. The Trump was on sale a few years later along with brands such as the Odeon, Little Artist, Opera, Music Teacher, Virtuoso, Federation and also the Dudley, made by the well-known accordion makers.

The True Tone was another arrival. Made for the British market, True Tone models were also popular in Australia in the 1930s and were described in their advertisements as 'the best in the world' and 'the acme of perfection' with 'no room for improvement'. Perhaps this implied that the True Tone would not be up-graded! In more detail, the models were described as:

'No. 1: *The baby mouth organ of the family and one of the best for its size.*

No. 2: *Very popular with good mouth organ players and very popular with the boys.*

No. 3: *Cannot be compared to any other mouth organ – made for sweetness, tone and quality.*

No. 4: *Two-sided in two keys, forty-reed model with solid nickelled covers.*

No. 5: *The most powerful mouth organ made and a real band in itself. Extra-large two-sided, two keys with forty-reeds.*'

Meanwhile, Mr and Mrs Hircoe who lived in Ascotvale, Melbourne were in court facing the judge. They lived next door to a church hall where meetings were regularly held. It would seem that this gathering of worshippers was so loud and enthusiastic in their hymn-singing that the noise and vibration occasionally caused a quantity of crockery to fall from Mrs Hircoe's kitchen shelf. By March 1922, the Hircoes could no longer cope and decided to hold a 'service' of their own in their back-yard, beside the church hall. Ernest Hircoe played his mouth organ at full volume while Mrs Hircoe played a whistle and banged on a piece of tin as they marched around their backyard. This unnerved the church gathering so much, that they immediately called the police. Constable Ryan later told the judge that on arrival at the church hall, he looked over the fence to see Hircoe and his wife walking around their yard playing a mouth organ and other instruments as 'loudly as possible' every time the church gathering started to sing hymns. Hircoe, already strained to the limit, had reached breaking point and screamed at the Constable to 'get off his fence!' He was fined forty shillings and twelve shillings costs but the case started a lot of discussion in the papers, with some for and some against the judge's decision.

One newspaper columnist, commenting on the case, wrote a humorous piece:

"For playing a mouth organ in his back-yard and disturbing a religious service next door, a man was fined forty shillings. That's what a volunteer organist gets for placing himself at somebody's service!"

Months later, after an appeal that discussed just what should define a church service, it was noted that although his conduct was 'unjustified', Hircoe was after all, on his own property. The conviction was quashed and Hircoe and his mouth organ won the day, without costs.

58 BOOMERANGS AND CRACKAJACKS

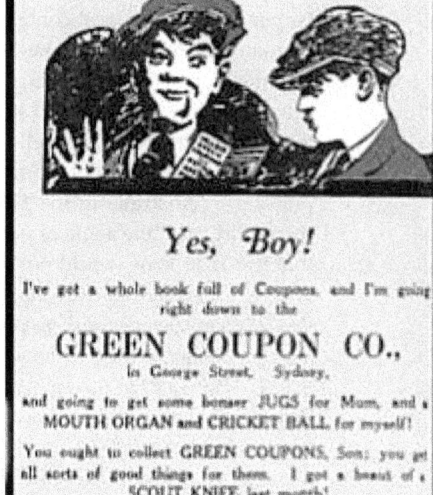

Vest Pocket miniature mouth organ with in-built high resolution magnifier

Canadian W.V. Robinson Weiss mouth organ promotion while on-tour in Australia in 1924

W. V. ROBINSON.

THE DARK SIDE OF THE MOUTH ORGAN

Around the end of the nineteenth century, gangs of youths made the streets of Australia's major cities a very unsafe place to be at night. In Sydney they stalked the streets of the inner-city areas from The Rocks to Woolloomooloo, committing some of the worst crimes imaginable, including some cases of murder.

Stand-over practices, robbery and constant brawling in these areas kept the residents ever alert and ready for trouble on most nights.

Known as the 'pushes', some gangs were less dangerous however and consisted of youths who simply got their kicks by intimidation, offensive language directed at passers-by and loud swearing in public.

It would appear that the favourite instrument of the pushes was the mouth organ, but these 'bands of players' were a far cry from the well-dressed, well groomed and very regimented young lads who were becoming a familiar part of the average mouth organ band of the time.

Weekends in the city's public places became known as dangerous 'hot-spots' as the two following reports by "The Argus" reveal.

On the Sunday afternoon of March 1923, ten seventeen-to-nineteen year olds were in the Melbourne Botanic Gardens playing mouth organs, singing 'rag-time' and playing two-up.

As they walked through the Gardens from the summer house to the lawns, they forced their way through anyone unfortunate enough to be passing 'and yelled objectionable remarks to women and girls'.

Three constables chased and arrested them but initially had no luck in identifying them, as they all gave the names of famous horse-racing jockeys.

By the time they had appeared in court a few weeks later however, true identities had been revealed and they were all fined forty shillings each.

On a summer's night on Melbourne's waterfront in February 1926, a push consisting of fifteen to twenty youths known as 'The Grey Caps' was walking down the street, taking up the whole of the footpath, 'calling out in a loud tone and singing'. One member of the group provided the accompaniment on a mouth organ.

When they saw the police approaching they dispersed quickly, except for one. The leader of the 'Grey Caps', Burt Neville, was known to the police and he later explained in court that their motto or creed was 'one run, all run'.

Just who was playing the mouth organ was not revealed but Neville did claim he was aware he was being watched by the law, or as he put it *"the police have got the knife in me"*.

60 BOOMERANGS AND CRACKAJACKS

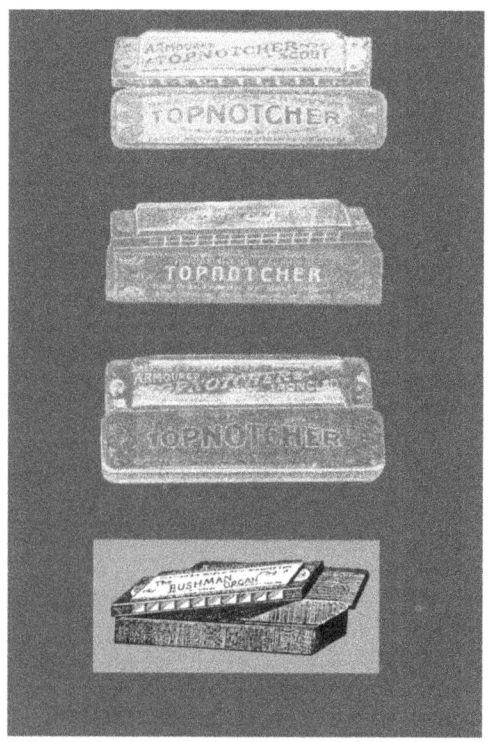

Another British-brand-name instrument, the Topnotcher, was a big seller in Australia from the early 1920s

Further reports by "The Argus" reveal that mouth organ theft was common in the 1920s. One example was a break-in at the shop of musical instrument dealer, Robert I. Smyth of South Melbourne in June of 1921. On a Sunday night, thieves smashed the glass window of his shop and made off with mouth organs, gramophone needles, records and other items.

The thieves that were after similar goods from the shop of William Henry Eutrope in Collingwood in February 1925, were however, more innovative. They got in through the back of the premises by cutting a hole in the rear wall. They stole one dozen mouth organs, an accordion, six portable gramophones, one dozen kazoos and some torches.

The Topnotcher, another mouth organ and also accordion line, for the British market was introduced in the early 1920s and sold well in Australia, giving further competition to a market that was by now dominated by the Boomerang, Crackajack and a whole variety of Hohners. The Topnotcher 'Armoured Ironclad' range was an indication by name alone, that this mouth organ was tough.

In Australia there were three models in this group, two twenty–reed types featuring 'incorrodible' reeds, metal reed cells, with nickel covers and available in strong metal cases. The Armoured Super Ironclad was similar, being a forty-eight-reed type available in a 'strong cardboard case.' Six other models were advertised along with another brand, The Bushman. It came in three models at 1/3d, 2/- and 4/6d.

The Topnotcher was widely promoted in Australia, to the extent that in 1925, W.H. Paling & Co. of Brisbane organised a Topnotcher Mouth Organ Championship, with gold medals and cash prizes at an Armistice Celebration Carnival. In the 1930s, Ernie Knight's Topnotcher Mouth Organ Band was popular and playing regularly around Melbourne.

Robberies 'of ' rather than 'by' mouth organs were much more common, but perhaps it was a Super Armoured Ironclad Topnotcher that was used as a shotgun in Melbourne in 1927, as reported by "The Argus" in August of that year.

Taxi-driver John Bond felt what he thought was a gun at the back of his head when he asked for the fare for conveying three male passengers from Coburg to Campbellfield, late on a Saturday night in August.

Bond raised his hands and the three fled the scene without paying, but he was quick in getting to the police station. Within less than an hour, the police were patrolling the area around Campbellfield and spotted and arrested the trio.

At Coburg Police Station, the men were searched for the weapon but all that was found was a mouth organ in one of the suspect's pockets.

It was verified that this instrument had been the 'weapon' used in the robbery and all three were duly charged.

62 BOOMERANGS AND CRACKAJACKS

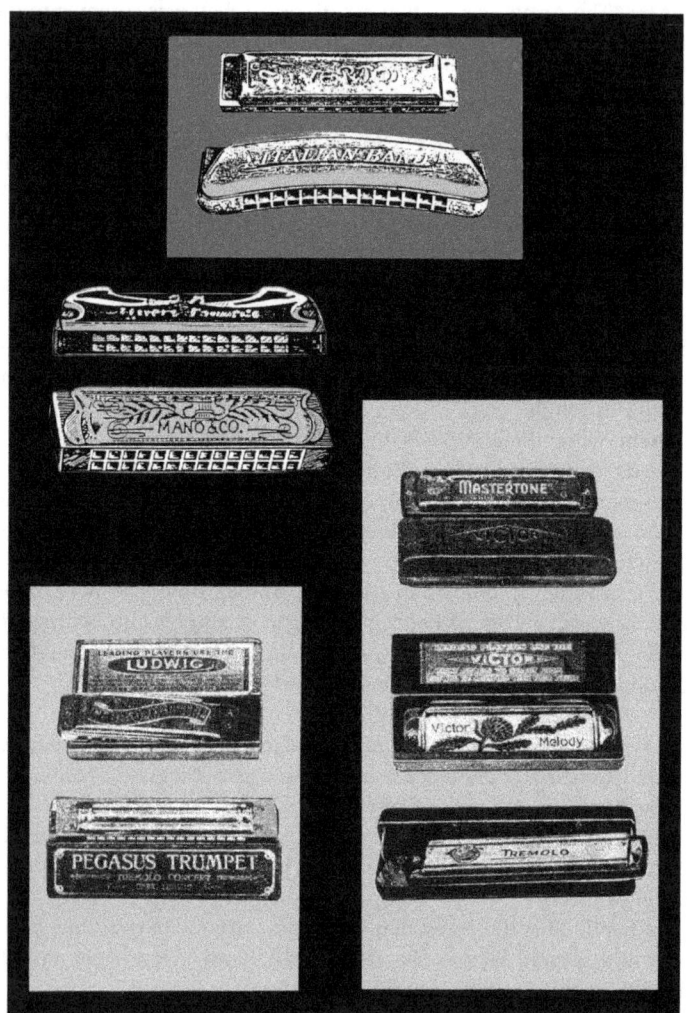

Italian, Swiss and German brands available in the 1930s to 1950s

It is difficult not to feel at least a little sorry for Hugh Ernst who was arrested for stealing a number of articles from his place of work, a warehouse in Melbourne.

In 1924, Ernst, who was a returned soldier, was battling to make ends meet, paying the rent and supporting his young daughter on a minimal wage. Someone at the warehouse got suspicious and called the police who intercepted him leaving work one afternoon. Searching his bag they found ten tins of sardines, a mouth organ and a few other articles he had taken illegally. Other items of interest were soon found when they searched his home as well.

Ernst explained to the court in November: *"I reside with a widow and two children and pay one pound a week rent. I have a little girl for whom I pay 12 shillings and 6d. a week. I am a returned soldier and have never been in trouble like this before"*

Regarding the stolen items he pleaded: *"I know I had no right to take them. I am only a poor man, struggling to get on. Do not make it too hard for me"*. Making no mention of the mouth organ, Ernst added: *"I will put the fish back"*. He was given a one month gaol sentence.

Perhaps a little bit of sympathy could also be extended to a young Melbourne musician who briefly went wrong for the sake of some mouth organs.

Auguste P. Fraillon, who in 1930 made about six visits to one of the city's top music houses, W. H. Glen Pty. Ltd. in Collins Street. In doing so, Fraillon had worked out an intricate plan to access Glen's huge stock of mouth organs.

On each occasion he entered the store as usual through the front door, took the lift to the third floor, then climbed out of a window and descended a ladder to where he could enter the warehouse section and proceed to fill-up a suitcase with the instruments.

He sold some of these to railwaymen, a few to a street musician and the rest to a tobacconist in a nearby suburb who was later questioned by the police.

After his arrest it was estimated Fraillon had stolen four hundred and fifty two mouth organs with a total value of fifty pounds. He claimed to have received only six pounds and eight shillings from the tobacconist.

In the courtroom in March, he suddenly 'burst into tears and collapsed on the floor of the dock'. After recovering he was given a three-month sentence, suspended for a two-year good-behaviour bond and placed under the care of the Salvation Army to straighten him out.

"The Canberra Times" reported a somewhat different crime, much later in December 1950, concerning young George Stevens who was in court in Sydney and about to be gaoled on the day before he was to be married. Possibly planning a little extra honeymoon money, he was charged with false pretences relating to fraudulently obtaining a railway ticket from which he received a refund.

While being questioned by Detective A.W. James, Stevens said; *"Let me play a tune on my mouth organ before I go to gaol?"* Detective James agreed to the request and Stevens played that old favourite and a very appropriate choice for someone in his situation: "Home, Sweet Home".

The Perla was introduced in 1926 as a new Australian brand-name mouth organ by Mick Simmons Pty Ltd.

It came in four types: the Medium 20-reed, the Medium Professional 20-reed, the Large 40-reed and the Large Professional 40-reed.

The Perla (pearler) an Australian term for 'the best' or 'something special', was described in 1920's advertisements as: *'Superior in every way in tone, quality and finish to any on the market. Embodying an entirely new principle of construction, the Perla is easy to blow, possesses a beautiful tone, sweet, vibratory and accurate and produces a perfect pianissimo and fortissimo'*.

In 1937, J. Albert & Son introduced the new Boomerang chromatic range and the last Boomerang diatonic, the Mezzo.

A lower-music-range model, the Mezzo was the perfect instrument for the band-member.

Allan & Co. replaced the Crackajack with a more modern, or up-to-date Australian brand-name in 1939: The Jazz Master.

The Hohner Company, having taken over most of the other German manufacturers, had a vast array of models available worldwide. Some were branded with American themes while others were styled for Europe.

Perhaps because of the problem that the Company had experienced with the Government over the Young Australia harmonica, they did not produce another specific Australian brand-name model. The Auto-Valve Harp range, which had been available internationally from around 1910, became the 'Australian Hohner' instead by 1930, for a market that was burgeoning due to the band movement and national competitions. They were taken up with even more enthusiasm by Australian players, both band members and soloists alike.

Back on the streets however, the instrument had been a part of some unfortunate situations over the years, as shown by a couple of isolated examples.

Mouth organist, Frank Davis was said to have been a 'friendly inoffensive sort of chap with fair hair, a slight build and rather good looking', who gave solo renditions in the pubs around Port Pirie in South Australia, reported the "West Australian" in November 1899.

He got into an altercation with a visiting seaman, Karl Svannson of Sweden, who did not appreciate his playing and demonstrated the fact by lunging at him with a knife, killing him almost instantly. The killer threw the knife away and ran off, but was eventually caught and charged with wilful murder.

"The Argus" covered case number two, where a mouth organ was only a part of the cause of a murder. In a North Melbourne residence in December 1930, a group of men had got together for a drink. They had consumed seven bottles of wine when an argument broke out between two of them, Josef Thur and another group member by the name of Prazenaca, who hurled a looking-glass and a mouth organ onto the floor, breaking the instrument into pieces. Thur picked up a broken piece of the mouth organ and hit it hard on a bed in the room which caused the situation to go completely out of control.

He left briefly and returned with a knife, when a third member, twenty seven year old Dezider Messerschmidt joined in the fight and was fatally stabbed.

Finally, a valediction: not an item about crime, but a fatal tragedy that happened to sixteen year old Sydney Elderfield of Melbourne in 1926.

Sydney was returning home with his brother to Coburg at around 9.30 pm from a picnic. The train had just left Box Hill station and was crowded, so Sydney stood near the carriage entrance and started playing his mouth organ.

Suddenly the train lurched a little, causing the door to fly open and Sydney fell backwards from the train, after which he was hit and killed by another coming in the opposite direction. *("The Argus" 27th January 1926).*

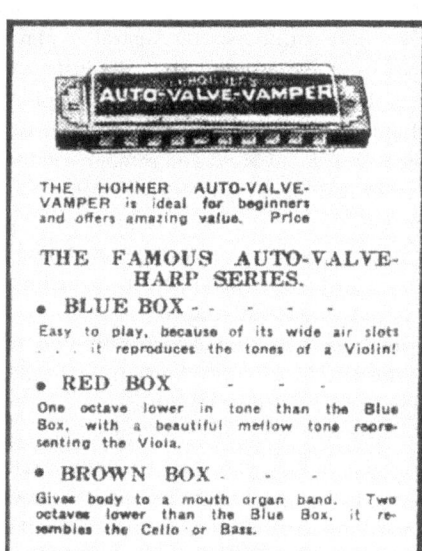

Hohner advertisements for the 'Australian' Auto-Valve Harp

Chapter Six

The Chromatic Harmonica and Another War

J. Albert & Son might have given some reassurance to anxious parents in the 1920s with their advertisement, advising that: *'If you teach a boy to blow a Boomerang he'll never blow a safe!'*
In fact, there were other alternatives to young players other than joining a push. Becoming a mouth organ band member was one of them.
After a band category was added to the annual South Street National Championships in 1929, hundreds of bands were formed all over Australia, a trend that was already under way in America and England. J. Albert & Son promoted the idea of school bands, with the eventual aim being a cup or a trophy award in a local competition, which could then lead to a state or even national win.
Throughout this period, various societies and institutions to help the underprivileged and needy were operating, providing both material and spiritual aid. A number of such institutions encouraged the use of the mouth organ with very worthwhile results. One example was the Melbourne Try Society, which stated in its magazine: "The Australian Boys Paper" that they did not exist only for those in need, but for 'boys of all classes who wished to further their general education and learn occupational skills such as carpentry, printing, typing and boot repairing'. The Try Society was not just responding to the current popularity of the instrument. They had been holding concerts for around twenty five years, featuring their young soloists and giving tuition and encouragement. In 1930, they held one of Melbourne's biggest mouth organ competitions. At their institution in South Yarra in 1933, at least four of Australia's national champion soloists and an equal number of bands, championship-winners included, competed. Among the competitors and winners, were a number of 'Try Boys', all expert players.
There is further proof that the mouth organ could be used for a good cause. In 1931, at Victoria's Geelong Gaol after a visit by a number of concert parties, The Geelong Mouth Organ Band, the first such band to make a record in Australia, paid visits and did charity work at the gaol. The prisoners were inspired to form a band of their own. A money collection pool was formed and with the funds collected, they installed an in-house wireless system throughout the prison with the permission of the authorities. After purchasing a receiver they managed to wire up most of the cells into which earphones were fitted and then, a loudspeaker was installed in the exercise yard.
A mouth organ band was formed and on-air concerts were given to the captive audience. Gaol authorities were said to be very happy with the results as it had cost the state nothing, but insisted that in the future, educational programs be included along with the mouth organ music.

68 BOOMERANGS AND CRACKAJACKS

The public school at Annandale, an inner Sydney suburb, was one of many that organised the formation of student mouth organ bands in the 1920s and 1930s with guidance from J. Albert & Son

Australian Champion Harold Collier in Melbourne training students for a future Crackajack Band

The Melbourne Boys Club Mouth Organ Band

Hohner's Kurt Jacob helped with the formation of a number of Hohner School Bands such as this outfit in Perth in the 1930s

THE CHROMATIC HARMONICA AND ANOTHER WAR 69

By 1933, The South Street Eisteddfod Society had afforded the mouth organ full honours, with the whole of the Opening Day's events taken up by competitions featuring the instrument.

The Victorian Mouth Organ Bands Association (VMOBA), in collaboration with the South Street Society, initiated a whole new program of competitions and large cash prizes along with an attractive array of cups and trophies which included the impressive Hohner Perpetual Shield.

The Geelong West City Harmonica Band, conducted by William Ketterer was Australia's most successful. They won numerous national events, toured interstate and made wireless broadcasts while The Malvern Tramways Harmonica Band of Melbourne conducted by Roy Ramage, came a close second in the same categories and activities.

The Geelong West City Harmonica Band

The Malvern Tramways Harmonica Band

70 BOOMERANGS AND CRACKAJACKS

*The Ballarat Ladies Mouth Organ Band at the Ballarat Benevolent Home
The performance was filmed by Fox-Movietone for a newsreel segment*

*The funeral of Thomas Harris
Victorian Mouth Organ Band Association President*

*Above Right and Right:
Harold Collier and the Melbourne Ladies Crackajack Mouth Organ Band.
The Funeral Procession and Church Service in Melbourne 1934*

The Victorian Mouth Organ Bands Association (VMOBA)

Below:
The Victorian Mouth Organ Band formed by the VMOBA to tutor and train the most promising young players in the late 1930s was short-lived due to the War. 1931 Australian Champion William Ketterer was Conductor and a young Horrie Dargie is far left, middle row

The call-up for World War II decimated the ranks of hundreds of mouth organ bands across the country and the subsequent shortage of mouth organs ensured that band activities came to an end for the older players as well. Only a few bands reformed after the War had ended. But strong ties had been formed and parting was not always easy, as Doug Wallace explained in his "History of The Rockhampton Mouth Organ Band" *(Rockhampton Historical Society 1985)*, when he said farewell to his band leader and conductor Jack Crossan, a Gallipoli veteran: *'It was a great experience and as with many great experiences, something had to happen, and it did. The drums of World War II had been beating strongly for some time and by now the message was in earnest. Most of us in early 1942 were by now no longer just lads and the call was there to be heard.*
One by one we joined the services, where we became pilots, mechanics, drivers, infanteers, machine-gunners and radio–operators. When I said goodbye I saw the look on his face that the others had seen, as they left for the army, navy or air force.
...this man that knew what it was all about showed that he knew what we were all about. And it showed too, that he had a clear sense of having achieved something worthwhile. He was tied to essential industry, and here was the end of a dream'.

72 BOOMERANGS AND CRACKAJACKS

Kurt Jacob and the first Australian Hohner agency in Flinders Street Melbourne 1937

The first 'slide' chromatics were marketed in Europe in the 1880s and even though a harmonica that offered the full musical scale was appreciated at the time, the mechanism of such an instrument would seem to have been too impractical.

In 1913, music dealers in Australia advertised 'Hohner's celebrated chromatic mouth organs' at 7/6d. each, without further specific mention of the actual model. It would appear that even straight-line type arrangement chromatics which were reasonably familiar in Europe, were rarely seen in this country.

Within ten years, a reliable slide-system had been perfected and a 10-hole, 40-reed model simply called the Hohner Chromatic Harmonica was available in Australia in the mid 1920s. The slide system was further refined, resulting in the introduction of the Hohner Chromonica range in the early 1930s.

THE CHROMATIC HARMONICA AND ANOTHER WAR 73

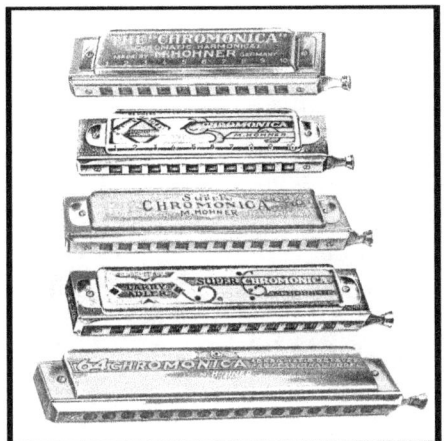

Hohner chromatic harmonica range:
Chromonica
Larry Adler Junior Chromonica
Super Chromonica
Larry Adler Super Chromonica
64 Chromonica

Below:
Vineta and Chromatica
chord accompaniment harmonicas

Top-selling Hohners in Australia in the 1930s to 1950s

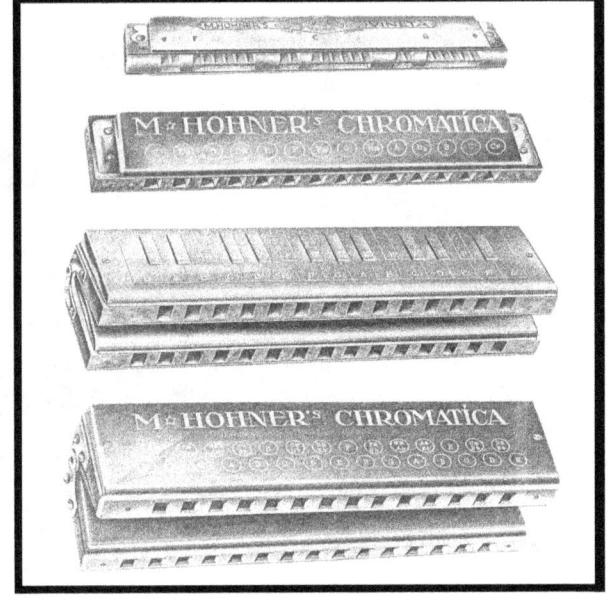

74 BOOMERANGS AND CRACKAJACKS

Popular in the U.S., the Borrah Minevitch brand was available in Australia in diatonic, chromatic and chord accompaniment models

On-sale in the 1930s and 1940s: The Radiotone chromatic. (Radiotone diatonics were also available in Australia)

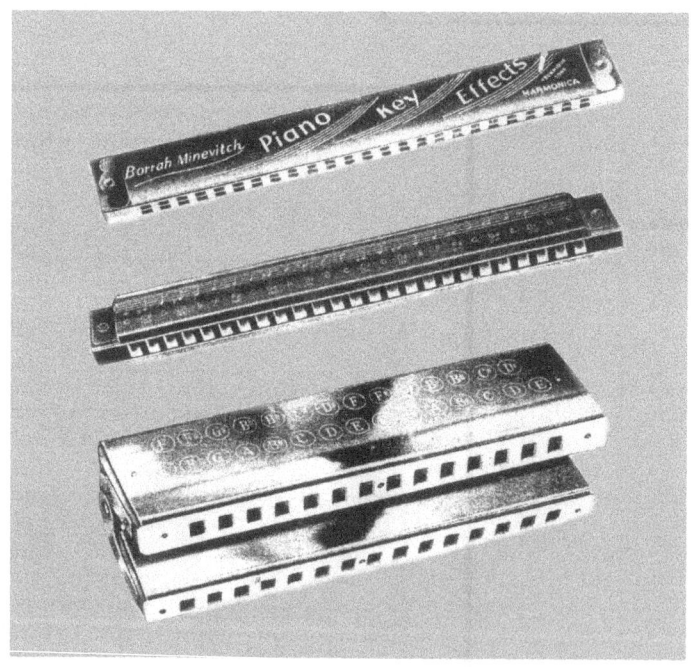

Aside from the Hohner range of chromatics and their large assortment of diatonic offerings, a few other brands made a brief appearance in Australia.

Chromatics were few and far-between, unable to compete with the Hohner because of the latter's patented and superior slide mechanism. However the extensive and stylish Borrah Minevitch range almost rivalled the Hohner models available, with two chromatic, and a range of chord models as played by the famous Harmonica Rascals. Four Minevitch diatonics were also available locally. Minevitch was a legendary player in America due to his recordings and movie appearances with The Harmonica Rascals. With nowhere near the same exposure in Australia, 'The Rascals' were still familiar through their short movie clips and recordings and were therefore, an inspiration to many Australian players.

The Radiotone brand was put on the market at the same time and comprised of three chromatics with 40, 48 and 64-reeds, and six diatonic models. The Rauner diatonic and chromatic harmonicas were also on sale in the mid 1930s, joined later by the Mancini chromatic and Claravox diatonics.

Some of the other brands that were in the shops from the late 1930s were the Leonora 20 and 40-reeds, the 20-reed Broadcast and a range of Soprani harmonicas. There were 24, 28 and 32-reed 'curved' models, double-sided 64, 80 and 96-reed types, a vamper and a tremolo.

Two chromatic 'Australian brands' were made available around this time; the Boomerang and the Crackajack. The Boomerang Chromatics in three types, the 40-reed Chromorgan, 48-reed Grand Chromorgan and 48-reed DeLuxe Chromorgan were introduced in 1937 and upgraded a few years later with improved embouchure holes and wind-economiser valves.

Crackajack Chromatics were introduced in 1938 in three similar types, but due to the World War II harmonica shortage and overwhelming competition from the Hohner brand, the entire Crackajack range was permanently discontinued. Allan & Co. briefly marketed the Australian brand-name, Jazz Master as a replacement.

Meanwhile, Larry Adler's American hit recordings and movie performances had ensured the world-wide popularity of the chromatic harmonica. He was the inspiration for countless performers from the mid 1930s and his first Australian visit in 1938-1939, resulted in a surge of harmonica sales not seen since the late 1920s. Many players now became more seriously engaged with the instrument, due to the ability to achieve the full musical scale and without having to resort to what some described as the 'tongue-twisting techniques' required on the diatonic instrument.

In Australia, Harry Thompson made the country's first chromatic harmonica recordings on a Hohner Super Chromonica in 1936, backing New Zealand country music star, Tex Morton. He then went on to record a series of solo medleys, producing a fresh, new and different sound compared to the diatonic offerings of the past. Horrie Dargie made his jazz debut on the Hohner Super Chromonica shortly after, as a member of Jim Davidson's Dandies, then formed the Rocking Reeds and made a series of further recordings as leader of the ensemble.

Both Harry Thompson and Horrie Dargie were involved in separate radio shows in the late 1930s. Thompson with Tex Morton as the Australian Hill Billys, made a series of programs for Macquarie Broadcasting titled "The Covered Wagon", an American-styled 'cowboy' presentation, while Dargie and his group starred in "The Shearing Shed Serenaders" for the ABC, an attempt to create a more Australian production. Judging by the following "Tempo" magazine review, '*Dargie got it right ... their object is, with the use of reeds, to create the real feeling and atmosphere of the 'outback' with presumably, the flavour of the shearing sheds. They succeed, mainly through the use of typical numbers.*'

Soon after, Thompson and Dargie joined the services along with so many other lesser known Australian mouth organists. Even Smilin' Billy Blinkhorn, who had emigrated from Canada only a year or so before, was off to war. He was a country music vocalist and guitarist who had just made a number of recordings at the Columbia studios in Sydney. One track, "The Wreck of the Old '97" featured his mouth organ playing and he continued a successful country music career in Australia after the war.

Eventually, all sorts of harmonica stories and myths were circulating through the Army, Navy and Air Force in the World War II period. One concerned a statement by Adolf Hitler himself, that he despised the mouth organ and considered it an instrument too lowly and humble for a nation such as Germany.

Another story came from a 'behind-the-scenes' member of the British War-Room who was surprised to see dozens of German-made mouth organs being purchased and delivered to the Chief-of-Staff. Further inquiries revealed that the top-brass were definitely not attempting to form a mouth organ band of their own. Instead, they were supposedly studying the locations of various factories in Germany from the intricate artwork on the mouth organ cover-plates and boxes, from which they could pin-point Allied bombing targets.

The 1940 Australian Champion, Eion S. Campbell, a Boer War and World War I veteran, experienced his third taste of battle in France in World War II, but this time as a correspondent, mainly for the "Whizz Bang" magazine.

The following is a small segment of his work from the "Whizz Bang" titled' 'The Last Post' in which Campbell describes a funeral march and the desolation of war:

'*Down the road that led to Beaulencourt, some infantry were marching…We followed in silence, slowly marching along the familiar road that led through the village, and past the leaning walls of plaster and debris of rafters and brickwork.*

And as the flowers nodded and smiled in the breeze, I thought of the legend that tells of flowers being the souls of soldiers that have died in battle. Many thousands of blossoms dotted the ruins and many thousands of khaki and grey soldiers lay among the trenches and shell craters beyond Beaulencourt and Le Transloy…'

THE CHROMATIC HARMONICA AND ANOTHER WAR 77

Left above:
Bentleigh Harmonica Band member Ron Gerrard
Left: Lt. Harry Thompson
Left below:
Horrie Dargie on-stage in New Guinea

Right above: Australian troops in Malaya
Right: A.I.F. - 1944 in Dutch New Guinea
Right below:
Northern Territory c.1941

78 BOOMERANGS AND CRACKAJACKS

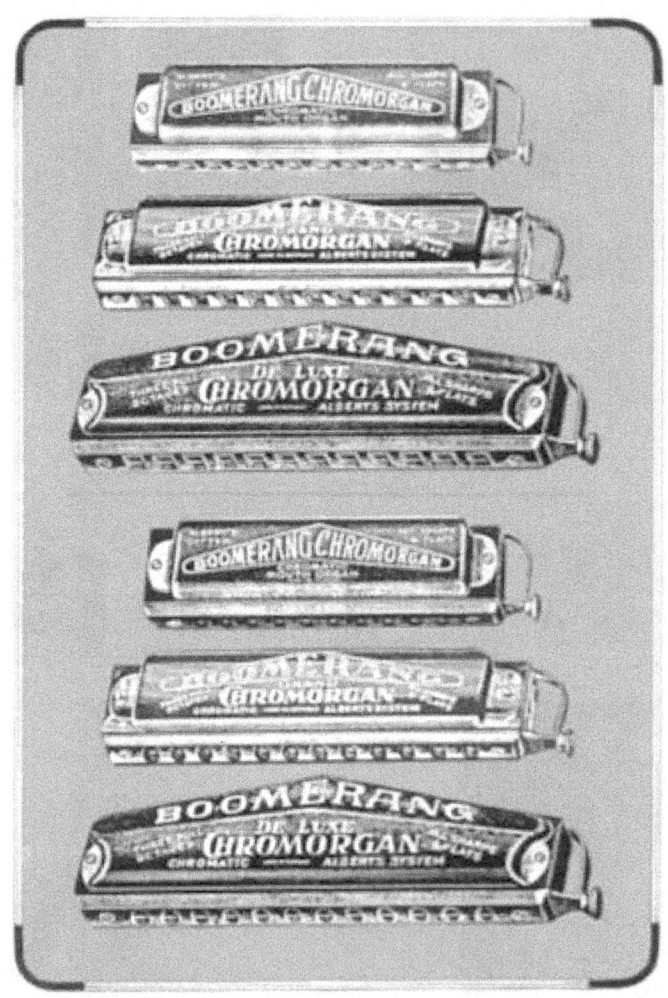

The J. Albert & Son Boomerang chromatic range introduced in 1937
Top: Chromorgan, Grand Chromorgan and DeLuxe Chromorgan
Bottom: Improved models introduced in 1940 all by Seydel (Germany)

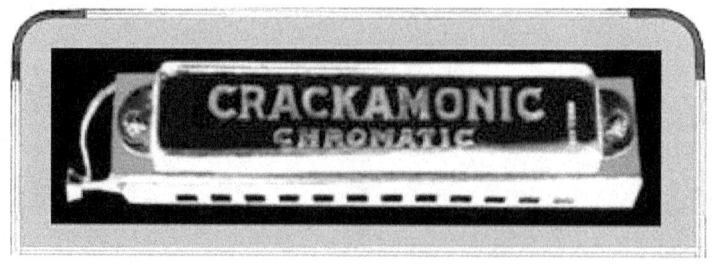

Allan & Co. introduced a similar chromatic range from 1937 -
the Crackamonic by Rauner (Germany)

Chapter Seven

The Professionals

After World War II, a new era for the harmonica in Australia began. The Boomerang instruments were by now the only Australian brand-name mouth organs on the market except for small plastic toy models in various colours, sold by stores such as Woolworths. These were the only mouth organs that were completely manufactured in Australia. The diatonic mouth organ was heard less, apart from the emerging folk music movement and the few remaining championships and bands were all but gone, but a new harmonica sound was emerging.

With the expanded musical possibilities introduced by the chromatic harmonica and international success by artists led by Larry Adler, the new harmonica music and style reached Australia just prior to the war, a style that was amply demonstrated by Horrie Dargie and his Rocking Reeds. The Horrie Dargie Quintet, a multi-instrumental and comedy act that featured the harmonica strongly, went on to achieve world-wide fame throughout the 1950s. In the Quintet's wake, numerous harmonica chromatic and chord instrument trios played clubs and restaurants all over the country and made countless television appearances.

The Hohner brand had become the top-selling harmonica in Australia, but things had not gone smoothly for Kurt Jacob. After moving from Melbourne to Sydney in 1948 he set up the agency, along with a musical instrument repair workshop in Bathurst Street. A year or so later, a tragedy almost occurred when the building caught fire. It was said to have started in the dark-room of an adjoining photographic studio when negatives caught alight, completely gutting the top eighth floor. Jacob and his only employee, Joseph Liphards were taken to Sydney Hospital and treated for serious cuts and burns. Jacob had in fact, been acknowledged as performing a heroic act by warning the building's hundreds of other occupants of the danger as the fire spread. Some ran through a sheet of flame reportedly four feet thick to escape the inferno but fortunately, no lives were lost.

Liphards claimed it took only thirty seconds or so after the initial warning before the whole workshop was ablaze and Jacob later discovered that the 'flight of stairs' he had used to desperately clamber down to the floor below, was in fact only a dangerously narrow railing, a fire escape being a feature that the building did not have at the time. The top floor was not re-built immediately after the fire, and Kurt Jacob & Co. decided to open a new Hohner office and showroom in Market Street, Sydney.

80 BOOMERANGS AND CRACKAJACKS

Fire rages through Kurt Jacob's Hohner showroom and musical Instrument workshop in Sydney
Top right:
In Trossingen, Germany, cases of Hohner harmonicas are packed and ready for shipment to Kurt Jacob & Co. in Sydney
Centre right:
Jacob attends the 1957 Hohner Centenary Celebrations in Trossingen, Germany.
Dr. Karl Hohner (centre) with Company members and Jacob (second left)
Right: Jacob talking to Mr and Mrs Ernst Hohner in Trossingen

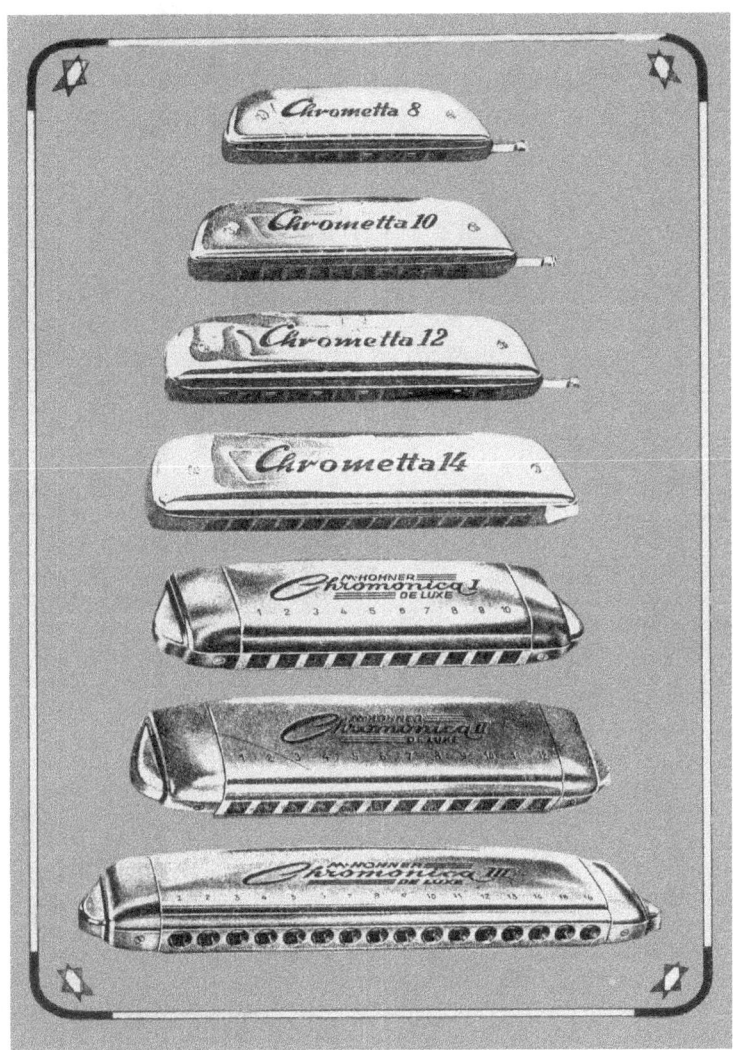

The Hohner Chrometta and Chromonica De Luxe range of chromatic harmonicas

82 BOOMERANGS AND CRACKAJACKS

*The famous Horrie
Dargie Quintet:
(from left:)
Reg Cantwell
Joe Hudson
Horrie Dargie
Vern Moore
'Doc' Bertram
and Kurt Jacob & Co.
Hohner advertisements*

*The Horrie Dargie
Quartet on the set
at ATV Melbourne:
(from left:)
Horrie Dargie
Billie Fowler
Vern Moore
'Doc' Bertram*

THE PROFESSIONALS 83

The Three Winds Trio (Sydney)

The Rhythm Reeds (Perth)

The Harmonichords (Brisbane)

The Hurricane Trio (Melbourne)

The Harmonicaires (Adelaide)

The Electrachords (Melbourne)

84 BOOMERANGS AND CRACKAJACKS

Hohner Educator, Comet and Golden Melody
A few examples of the many Hohner diatonic harmonicas available in Australia through the 1950s and 1960s

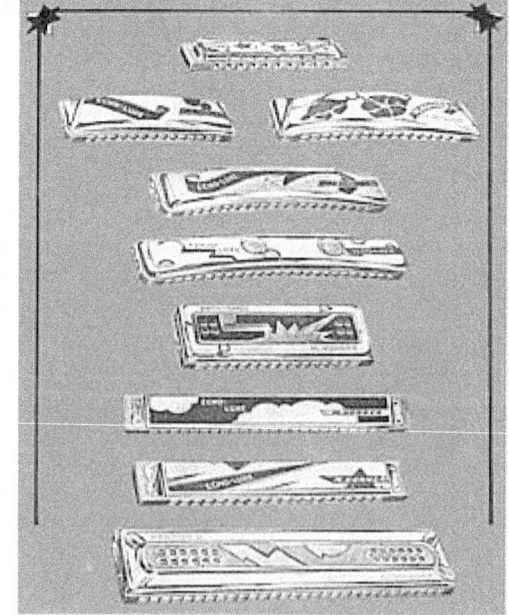

The Hohner Echo-Luxe range

THE PROFESSIONALS

Celebrating the release of "Bluegene's Boogie"

James and Joan Jimae toured their act from the U.S. on the Tivoli circuit during 1953 and 1954. Joan was born in Australia and had worked as a Tivoli performer.
In 1953 their son Gene recorded eight tracks at Sydney's Columbia studios for four 78rpm disc releases with Bob Gibson an his Orchestra.
Gene - 'a child prodigy' - had been playing harmonica professionally since the age of five in the U.S.
After their return to America an album titled "Harmonica Magic" was released.
Gene died in a car crash in Miami aged eighteen and James and Joan eventually retired in Australia.

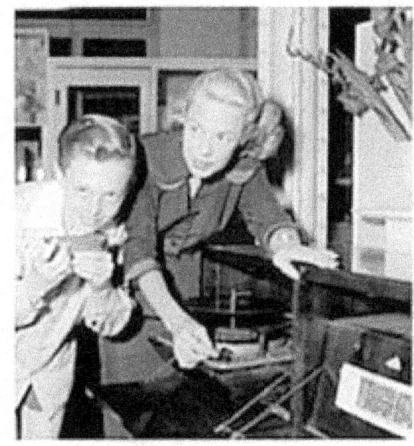

Fans gather around at the recording launch
Right: Gene and his mother Joan

Bruce Skurray (Sydney)

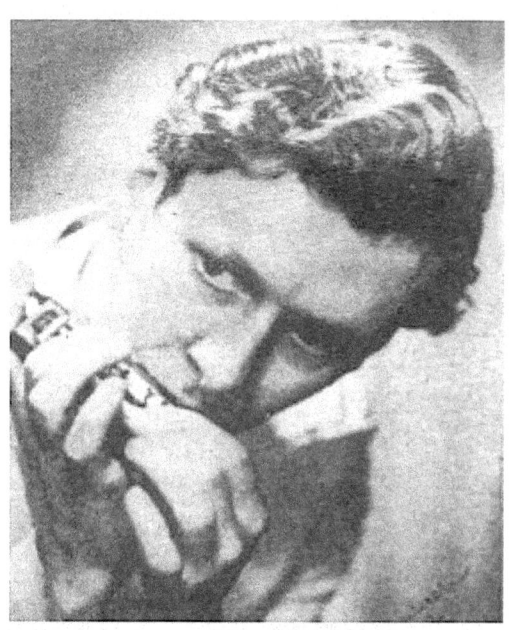
Laurie Smith (Brisbane)

Peter Thompson (Hobart)

Vic de Lano (Perth)

THE PROFESSIONALS 87

The Horrie Dargie Quintet arrive back in Australia in 1958 after their five-year world-tour

Robert Leeman left Australia in 1956 for a twelve-month tour of England, Canada and Italy
Below left: Leeman on the BBC in London
Below right: Performing at the "Carols by Candlelight" Christmas Concert in Melbourne after losing his sight due to a brain tumour in 1967 and at home in Melbourne, with his guide dog and companion, 'Sandy'

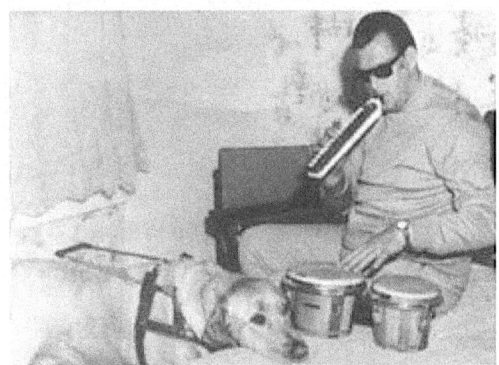

88 BOOMERANGS AND CRACKAJACKS

American Herb Schreiner toured here in 1939. He made his Hollywood movie debut in "Main Street to Broadway"

U.S. visitors in the 1960s: John Sebastian (Left), and Stagg McMann (Above)

Larry Adler drives the 1904 Darracq, 'Genevieve' on his arrival at Brisbane Airport for his 1961-62 nation-wide tour. Adler wrote the theme for the English movie which became one of his best-selling recordings. At the time 'Genevieve' was owned by Gilltrap's Auto Museum on Queensland's Gold Coast

Below:
1950s advertisements for 3 inch plastic mouth organs, available in various colours and manufactured in Australia

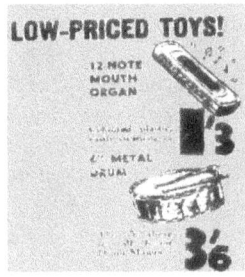

Above: The last J. Albert & Son Boomerangs in 1949: Swiss-manufactured Chromorgan and Grand Chromorgan

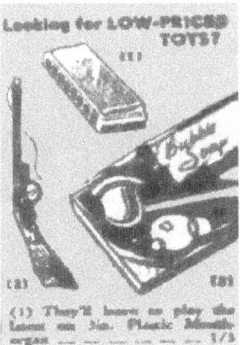

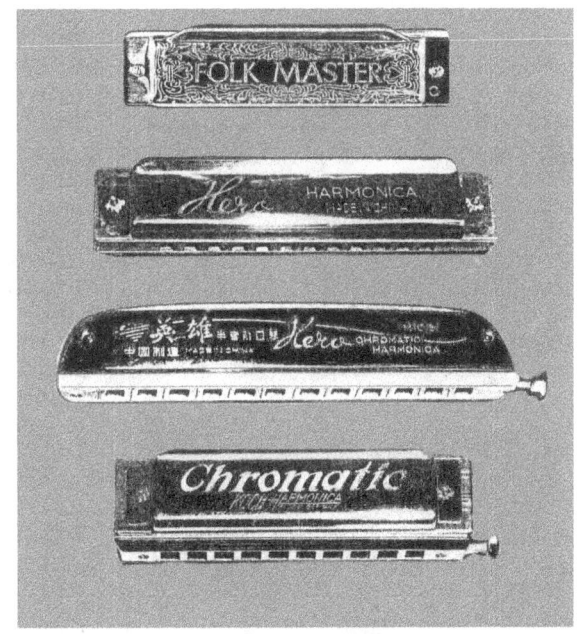

Japanese Folk Master (diatonic) Chinese Hero (diatonic and chromatic) German Koch Chromatic. On-sale in Australia 1950s to 1970s

Performances by visiting overseas chromatic players and television and club spots by highly-professional local artists significantly raised the status of the instrument. The basic diatonic mouth organ would however, continue to hold a very important place in the hearts and minds of most Australians. For Americans, the instrument conjured up visions of the Civil War or the cowboy on the prairie, while the Australian image was that of the drover, miner, shearer or squatter camped in the bush around an evening fire.

Less than a decade before the advent of the chromatic harmonica, author, F.D. (Frank Dalby) Davison captured this image in his book, "Forever Morning":

'...In shearing sheds and wayside shanties, in cattle camps and at bush dances, it is the melodist with his mouth organ who enlivens the passing hour. He mostly plays by ear; his repertoire is astonishing both in length and variety; and somehow the wailing reeds and the throbbing vamp which the musician knows how to draw from his instrument fit the Australian scene exactly. Given a small campfire at the foot of gum trees that reach up to a star-shot sky; a solitary figure seated on his unrolled swag before the flames, the plaintive reeds filling the night with strains of "Drink to Me Only", and you have a scene at which passing Pan might pause to peer and listen'.

("Forever Morning" (An Australian Romance) by F.D. Davison – Published by Australian Authors Publishing Company 1931)

Left: The diatonic instrument in Australian folk music
The Bushwhackers in the play "Reedy River" in 1953
Harry Kay on mouth organ
Below left: The Bushwhackers perform at Sydney Showground 1955

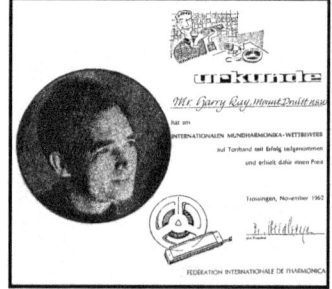

Harry Kay was a prize-winner in a 1962 German Harmonica Competition with entries judged by tape

Left to Right:
E.S. Campbell, *program sponsor Mr Hughes, Laurie Smith, announcer Noel Horn and Eddie Edmonds at the 4KQ 1954 Queensland Mouth Organ Championship*

Eddie Edmond's 1954 Mouth Organ Club Grand Christmas Concert at Kurilpa Town Hall Brisbane

In Brisbane, a club that catered for mouth organ players only, had been in operation from the early 1930s. Eddie Edmonds (Eddie the Boomerang Mouth Organ Man), a 1927 Queensland Champion, operated his Mouth Organ Club on 4BC and 4KQ and taught over twenty thousand students through his studios and as part of a Queensland schools program. He held regular concerts, had a weekly radio show and in the early days of television, made an appearance with club members.

Edmonds was responsible for the last championship in Australia, an on-air Queensland State Competition in 1954. Sharing the microphone on that day were two Queensland mouth organ legends: Eion S. Campbell, the recording artist, Queensland Champion and 1940 Australian Champion, and Laurie Smith, the state's best known chromatic harmonica player, famous for his stage, radio and television appearances from the 1950s.

With his brother Rex, another popular Brisbane player, Smith also leased and operated the Theatre Royal and presented a weekly program of some of the last vaudeville shows in Australia. Needless to say, Smith featured many harmonica performances at the Royal, an old theatre that had some mouth organ history of its own, being the aforementioned venue for the Hedley-Hunt two-man mouth organ challenge of 1910. (See page 39).

The Mouth Organ Club in a 1956 street procession in Brisbane

The Abercrombie Caves are situated near the western New South Wales town of Trunkey Creek, about sixty kilometres from Bathurst. The main part of the cave system is a large cavern known as the Grand Arch, said to be the greatest natural tunnel in the world.

Around 1860, a dance floor or stage was built inside the Grand Arch by local gold-mining communities as a gathering place for entertainments and music concerts. In 1880, a new stage was built on the site of the old one and stands to this day. Around 1950 after a flood swept through the Caves, a number of small implements and musical instruments were unearthed from beneath the stage platform, including the remains of a Japanese Butterfly Harmonica. The harmonica relic has occasionally been put on display at the Abercrombie Caves Resort.

Established in 1887, the Nippon Musical Instrument Company is the manufacturer of the Butterfly harmonica and a range of other instruments. The Butterfly was popular in Australia, helped to some degree by an unusual concert at Sydney Town Hall in 1926.

The harmonica band from the visiting Japanese naval training ship, "Taisei Maru", presented selections from "Carmen", Bizet's "L'Arlesienne" and works by Lubormisky and Waldteufel. Diatonic harmonicas with chord accompaniment models were used, possibly the first time that such arrangements had been heard in Australia.

The Butterfly harmonica unearthed from beneath the stage at the Abercrombie Caves

After 1979, concerts of classical, country, folk, rock, jazz and blues were held regularly on the stage, drawing huge crowds. Leading Australian actor, Jack Thompson who paid his harp-playing dues in a 1960s Brisbane band, gave performances there, starting with the 1988 "Blues from the South" Concert in which he took part.

Jack Thompson at the "Blues from the South Concert"

THE PROFESSIONALS 93

Actor Simon Burke recalls memories of his late father and his mouth organ in the film "The Irishman"

There have been some memorable mouth organ moments in Australian cinema since Maggie Moore's 'silent' performance of "Home, Sweet Home" in "Struck Oil" in 1920.

On his 1962 visit, Larry Adler made his second Australian recording with "The Theme from 'They Found a Cave'" and "Journey's End", two Peter Sculthorpe compositions recorded for the film, which were also released on an HMV single.

Donald Crombie's 1978 feature, "The Irishman" had the instrument as a strong part of the storyline, while an earlier Crombie film, "Caddie" (1976), contained brief sequences.

Chris Noonan's "The Riddle of the Stinson" was released in 1987 starring Jack Thompson in an award-winning role. It featured the music and blues harp of Jim Conway.

The outback scene in the 2008 Baz Lurhmann film epic "Australia", in which Thompson takes his 'J. Albert & Son Boomerang mouth organ' from his pocket and plays, is another 'moment' that will be long-remembered. The harmonica soundtrack is credited equally to Thompson, Conway, Lawrie Minson and David Hirschfelder, and in the movie storyline the Boomerang Grand itself becomes a part of Australian Indigenous culture, when it is passed on to a young Aboriginal boy, 'Nullah', played by Brandon Walters.

Hohner diatonic and chromatic harmonicas
Blues Harp,
Special 20
Meisterklasse ,
Larry Adler Professional 12,
Silver Concert Chromonica,
Super 64 Chromonica

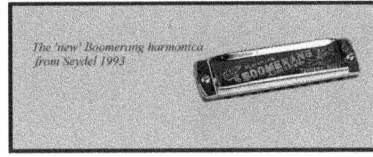

By the 1970s, some of the chromatic players from previous decades had established successful careers in television, movie and session work, music arranging and the occasional club appearances, notably Richard Brooks, Lionel Easton and Horrie Dargie. In his later years, Dargie played regularly on cruise-ships that travelled to island destinations around the Pacific Ocean.

He was engaged for solo performances on the East German-built Russian liner "Mikhail Lermentov" in February 1986, when it hit a reef off Cape Jackson in New Zealand's Queen Charlotte Sound. It happened in driving rain, late on a Sunday afternoon.

By 11.00 pm that night, the 20,352 tonne liner had gone down with the last of more than seven hundred passengers and crew (except for one missing crewman), having been rescued only minutes before and taken ashore by a flotilla of various craft that had come to their aid.

All of Dargie's belongings, harmonicas included, were lost and "The Sydney Morning Herald" report of the passengers' return to Sydney included a photograph of a lady survivor who had been reminiscing with Horrie and his wife Cathy, on board just prior to the sinking. They had just met and had been talking about old-time harmonica players. In a remarkable coincidence, she was Eleanor Martyn, a sister of pioneer recording artist, Harry Thompson.

Horrie Dargie and his harmonica collection

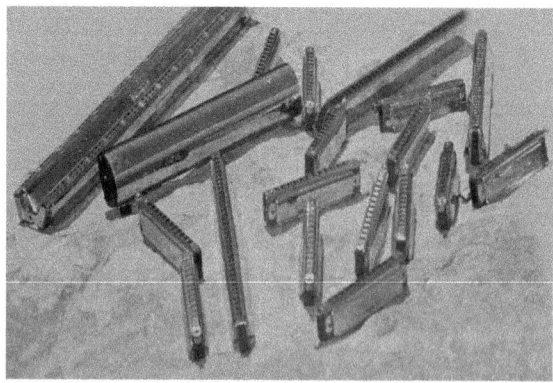

Chapter Eight

Mouth Organ Memorabilia

1920s Sydney shop window Boomerang display

Above: Thomas & Co., an inner-Sydney suburb music shop c.1920 with facade advertising for Rexophone Records, Dominion Accordions and Cobber mouth organs

On-sale in 1906: Markneukirchen Sachsen mouth organ with bells sold for 3/9d, post free

On-sale in Australia in 1913- 1920: Trumpet Harmonica, Famous Dancing Harp Harmonica and Herold & Son two-bell mouth organ for 2/3d (also available- one-bell model for 1/6d.)

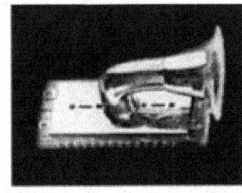  

Boomerang mouth organ display cases for music-shop retailers:
Above: Junior Cabinet
Right: Large Cabinet

Above: Retailer's portable display box

The ultimate in mouth organ memorabilia: the 1925 Packard Holebrook-bodied coupe which was purchased new by Frank Albert, straight off the floor of a New York motor show exhibit, on one of his many overseas visits. Albert had the car converted to RHD and brought to Australia, where he had a Boomerang mouth organ replica mounted on the bonnet-front as a mascot. Thought to be one of only two still in existence world-wide, the car was discovered in the 1970s on a New South Wales farm by collector and restorer, Neville Fisher and is now owned by Alison Griffiths of Victoria

Home, Sweet Home: The House That Dick Robertson Built

In 1911, Dick Robertson (1886-1960), a brilliant exponent of the Boomerang miniature mouth organ, took part in a two man contest at the Protestant Hall in Queanbeyan, New South Wales against H.R.'Dick' Shalder (1884-1953), a professional Boer War soldier, trumpeter and mouth organ player. Shalders had recently arrived from duties in India and South Africa, transferring his military career to Australia, where he initially became a horse-riding instructor at Duntroon in Canberra. Shalders' claim that he 'had never been beaten in mouth organ contest' was justified when he won by just eight points in an exhausting event which required the two contestants to perform seven separate tunes, out of sight of the judge. Shalders and Robertson concluded the evening with a moving duet of "Annie Laurie", but Robertson then went on to 'win the night' by performing a mouth organ solo and step-dance at the same time.

In 1912, Dick and Mary Robertson began building their house at Oaks Estate, originally a small rural-suburb of Queanbeyan, bordering the area that had been declared part of the Australian Capital Territory when the city of Canberra began to take shape. As the Robertson family grew over the years, Dick, a plumber by trade, made additions by hand to enlarge and improve the dwelling and small farm, while he worked on the government buildings of Canberra and became known locally as 'the mouth organ king'. Although his talent was recognised by Columbia in Sydney, his exceptional 1932 Parlophone recording of "Home, Sweet Home"/"Red Wing", was soon forgotten, mainly due to the Depression. In 1937 an accident while working on Government House ("Yarralumla"), left him permanently incapacitated.

After his death, his son Les lived in the house for thirty years or so, after which it fell into disrepair until its heritage value was recognised and classified by the National Trust and restoration work commenced. **'The house is the last example of a worker's shanty left in the ACT. It was built in stages using make-shift building materials including bush poles, flattened kerosene tins, flat iron off-cuts, packing case boards and weather boards. Some materials were off-cuts from construction jobs in early Canberra, including the provisional Parliament House. The sheds in the yard were used as a cookhouse and sleep-outs at various times'.** (Canberra Archaeological Society)

The Robertson house, now held in higher regard than at any other time in its humble one-hundred year existence, was witness to five decades of his life and mouth organ music and is still standing strong. Meanwhile, one of the many government buildings on which Robertson plied his trade, The Institute of Anatomy, has long-since been transformed into The National Film and Sound Archive and houses a copy of his rare 1932 recording, so aptly titled: "Home, Sweet Home".

98 BOOMERANGS AND CRACKAJACKS

*Left:
Earliest-known mouth organ
recordings made in Australia:
"Mouth Organ Medley"
and "Mouth Organ Medley No. 2" by
Professor Dickens. Cylinders released
c. 1908 on Empire Records*

*The first Australian mouth organ disc
recording: "The Prisoner's Song" by
P.C. Spouse, released 1927 on Regal*

*Australia's best-selling mouth organ
record in the period: "Anvil Chorus"
by P.C. Spouse, released in 1928*

*First Australian mouth organ band
record: "Under the Double-Eagle"
by the Geelong Mouth Organ Band
in 1929*

*"Mouth Organ Medley" by the North
Sydney Tramway Mouth Organ Band
released in 1935*

MOUTH ORGAN MEMORABILIA 99

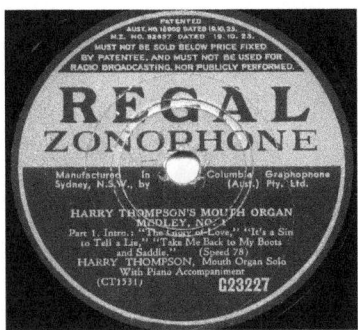

The first solo chromatic harmonica recordings made in Australia in 1937: "Harry Thompson's Mouth Organ Medleys"

Horrie Dargie and His Rocking Reeds recording of "Waltzing Matilda" released in 1941

Above:
Larry Adler's 1939 release of "Hungarian Rhapsody", recorded in Australia with Jim Davidson and the ABC Dance Band
Above Right:
Gene Jimae's Australian recording of "Bluegene's Boogie" with Bob Gibson and his Orchestra in 1953
Right:
The Hohner Accordion Symphony Orchestra rendition of "Waltzing Matilda" recorded in Australia in 1955 with Rolf Glass on harmonica

100 BOOMERANGS AND CRACKAJACKS

J. Albert & Son Boomerang mouth organ tutors from the early 1900s to 1949

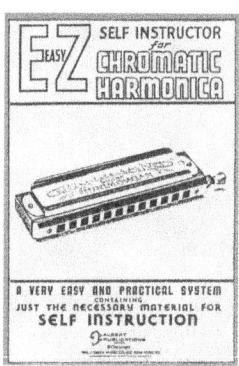

MOUTH ORGAN MEMORABILIA 101

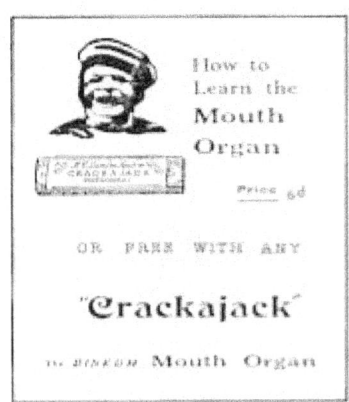

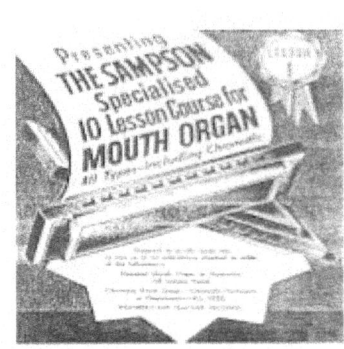

Thousands Have Tried to Teach Themselves and Have Failed.

THE GODFREY COLLEGE OF MUSIC, 111 GEORGE STREET, SYDNEY, through the WONDERFUL METHOD invented by our Director, GUARANTEES to teach the MOUTH-ORGAN SUCCESSFULLY from real music by post. Even if you have never learnt music before, you will play tunes from the first lesson. We are so sure of your success that we will lend you A CELEBRATED MOUTH ORGAN, A GLAZ-O-PHONE MOUTHPIECE, A TIME BEATER, TIME INDICATOR, and NOTE INDICATOR, for THREE MONTHS FREE OF CHARGE.

This wonderful Glaz-o-Phone Mouthpiece enables you to give a true imitation of the VIOLIN, CHRISTY ORGAN, CHURCH ORGAN, VIBRATO, GLISSANDO, VOX-HUMANA, BUGLE CALLS, BRASS BANDS, etc. You are under no agreement. We will trust you with the above-mentioned complete outfit for THREE MONTHS FREE OF CHARGE.

THE GODFREY COLLEGE OF MUSIC

Australian mouth organ tutors from the early 1900s

102 BOOMERANGS AND CRACKAJACKS

*Above and right:
Gold-plated Hohner Marine Band and trophies won by Australian Champion Waldo Burgoyne in the 1930s*

Official badge as worn by Members of the Malvern Tramways Harmonica Band

'Dummy' Boomerang used for advertising and as a stage-prop in comedy acts

Framed 1930 photograph of The Geelong Mouth Organ Band donated to The National Film & Sound Archive Canberra by Ray Grieve on behalf of band-member Eddie Wakefield

Chapter Nine

Harmonica Legends Reunited

The initial planning and research for "A Band in a Waistcoat Pocket", including the collection of all the known recorded music, started in 1981. After more than ten years of researching, collecting material and interviewing players or their descendants from all around Australia, the task of compiling and writing began. Part of the collection process included the acquisition of every known mouth organ record made in Australia up to the 1940s featuring the harmonica as the lead instrument.

Transferring the old and sometimes extremely rare and fragile items to a professional level of sound-quality on tape was undertaken by Chris Long, Melbourne media historian, audio and film consultant and researcher. He transferred the cylinder records to tape with his electric phonograph player machine, specially constructed for cylinder-to-tape transfers and unique at the time. Chris has since then significantly upgraded his equipment for such tasks.

The National Film and Sound Archive (NFSA) in Canberra undertook the task of doing the same with the 78 rpm disc records, and a master tape was produced by audio and sound technician Ian Gilmour. The book itself was the end product, written with invaluable editing assistance from Jacqueline Kent and published by Currency Press in 1995. A self-published four hour, 4-volume tape set titled "Australian Harmonica History" was also released. Approximately three hours of this set was then made available in CD form by Warren Fahey, issued as a 2 CD set on his Larrikin label also titled "A Band in a Waistcoat Pocket". This CD set was released as a companion to the book and re-issued in 2002 as part of Warren Fahey's 'Yesterday's Australia' series.

Larry Adler, who was on tour in Australia at the time, officially launched the book and CD Set in 1995 at the Hotel Intercontinental in Sydney. The book launch also served as reunion for a large gathering of players and their descendants from various parts of Australia, bringing them together for the first time in many years. It had been fifty years for Larry Adler and Horrie Dargie.

Left: Chris Long transfers the Professor Dickens cylinders to audio tape

Right: Ian Gilmour producing the master tape at the National Film & Sound Archive

The launch of "A Band in a Waistcoat Pocket" at the Hotel Intercontinental Sydney, May 1995

Top: Katharine Brisbane of Currency Press
Above left: Warren Fahey (Larrikin Records)
Above: Larry Adler performs "Summertime"
Left: Author Ray Grieve

Above:
Christian Marsh with Hohner distributors Tricia and Jac Smits. Smit's Music kindly gave mementos of miniature Hohner harmonicas to the assembled guests

Above right:
Richard Brooks and Kurt Jacob

Right:
Ray Grieve (centre) and a media journalist listen to Nellie Collier (widow of Harold), talk about her days with The Melbourne Ladies Crackajack Mouth Organ Band

Right:
Larry Adler tells a joke to Adler tour promoter Andrew McKinnon, Ray Grieve and Nellie Collier

106 BOOMERANGS AND CRACKAJACKS

"A Band in a Waistcoat Pocket" Currency Press Book Launch May 1995:
From left:
Bruce Skurray,
Larry Adler,
Ray Grieve,
Harry Kay,
Jim Conway,
Richard Brooks,
Horrie Dargie

Bruce Skurray, Larry Adler, Ray Grieve, Jim Conway, Nellie Collier, Richard Brooks, Horrie Dargie. Adler and Dargie meet again: Their first reunion since they entertained the World War II troops in New Guinea

INDEX

Adler, Larry 75, 79, 88, 93, 99, 101, 103, 104, 105, 106
Albert, Frank 19, 42, 43, 50
Albert, J. & Son 2, 17, 18, 19, 20, 22, 23, 24, 30, 38, 39, 44, 45, 46, 47, 50, 64, 67, 68, 78, 89, 93, 100, 102
Allan & Co. 20, 21, 22, 36, 47, 48, 49, 50, 64, 75, 78, 95, 96, 101
Allan, George Clark 20, 21
Andrews, Stan 47
Annandale Boomerang Mouth Organ Band 68
Aronson, Joe & his Orchestra 44
Australian Hill Billys 76
Ball, William 3
Ballarat Harmonica Band 50
Ballarat Ladies Mouth Organ Band 70
Ballarat South Street Committee 50, 51, 51, 69
Bell, Alexander Graham 10
Bertram, 'Doc' 82
Besses O' Th' Barn 22
Bishop, Henry Rowley 6
Bilger, Johannes 4
Blackman, Mr 4
Blinkhorn, Smilin' Billy 76
Blyth, Edna 50
Boath, A. 37
Bob Gibson Orchestra 99
Bohm, F.A. 46
Bond, John 61
Boon & Co. 4
Borrah Minevitch Harmonica Rascals 75
Bowen, Sir George 9
Boys Brigade Harmonica Band 20, 22
Brisbane, Katharine 104
Brooks, Richard 94, 105, 106
Burgoyne, Waldo 53, 102
Burke, Simon 93
Bush Music Club 90
Bushwhackers 90
Neville, Burt 59
Butler, D. 37
Campbell, Eion S. 51, 51, 76, 91
Cannwell, Reg 82
Carter, W. 4
Castles, Amy 34
Chisholm, Alexander H.
Clark, G.F. 101
Clark, Lillian 50
Collier, Harold 49, 50, 68, 70, 105
Collier, Nellie 105, 106
Conway, Jim 93, 106
Coxon, W.F. & Co. LTD 16
Crackajack Band 34

Crackajack Orchestra 49
Cracknell, Superintendent 10
Crombie, Donald 93
Crossan, Jack 71
Currency Press 103, 104, 105, 106
Dargie, Cathy 94
Dargie, Horrie 71, 75, 76, 77, 79, 82, 94, 101, 103, 106
Davis, Frank 65
Davis, J.W. 4
Davison, F.D. 90
Deane, Mr 3
De Lano, Tic 86
Dickens, Charles 42
Dickens, Sydney 42, 45, 52
Domasco, B. 37
Donnelly, James 25
Easton, Lionel 94
Edmonds, Eddie 91
Egmont Band 17
Elderfield, Sydney 65
Electrachords 83
Emmet, Joseph K. 8, 9
Emmett, Albert 25
Ernst, Hugh 63
Errol Street State School Crackajack Band 53
Eutrope, William Henry 61
F.A Bohm 21
Fahey, Warren 103, 104
Faye, Phyllis 39
Feldheim, Gotthelf & Co. 40
Fell, Johannes 4
Fischer, Vincenz 4
Forrest, A.W. 53
Forstner, Joseph 4
Fowler, Billie 82
Fraillon, Auguste.P. 63
Franklin, Sir John 5
Franklin, Lady 5
Geelong Mouth Organ Band 67, 95, 102
Geelong West City Harmonica Band 51, 69
Gerrard, Ron 77
Gilmour, Ian 103
Glass, Rolf 99
Glier, Johann Wilhelm 4
Godfrey College Mouth Organ Course 101
Greaves, Joseph 5
Grieve, Ray 43, 103, 104, 105, 106
Haffner, Martin 3, 4
Hambleton, S.E. 34
Harmonicaires 85

Harmonichords 55
Harris, Thomas 70
Hartig, Michael 4
Hedley, Tom 39, 91
Hill, Alfred 38
Hill, Police Magistrate 17
Hircoe, Ernest 57
Hirschfelder, David 93
Hitler, Adolf 22, 76
Hoffnung & Co 40
Hohner Accordion Symphony Orchestra 99
Hohner Company 47, 51, 65, 66, 72, 79, 80
Hohner, Dr. Karl 80
Hohner, Mr and Mrs Ernst 80
Hohner School Band 68
Hollis, Mr 5
Horn, Noel 91
Horrie Dargie Quartet 82
Horrie Dargie Quintet 79, 82, 87
Horrie Dargie Rocking Reeds 75, 79, 98
Hordern, William 3
Hosking, Ernest 15
Hotz, Friedrich 4, 12
Howard's Music Warehouse 40, 41
Hudson, Joe 82
Hunt, George 39, 91
Hurricane Trio 55
Infant School Society 5
Jackson & McDonald 25, 26
Jackson, Samuel 25
Jacob, Kurt 47, 51, 65, 72, 79, 80, 105
Jennings, Leslie 51
Jim Davidson ABC Dance Band 99
Jim Davidson's Dandies 75
Jimae, James, Joan, Gene 85, 99
Kay, Harry 90, 106
Kent, Jaqueline 103
Ketterer, William 69, 71
Kissling, Jacob 4
Kopech, Gustavo 10
Kurt Jacob & Co. 79, 80, 82, 97
Lacy, George 55
Langhammer, Johann 3
Langwarrin Army Training Camp 31
Lazar, Miss 5
Lindenmuller, Hans 3, 4
Liphards, Joseph 79
Little Miss Kookaburra 52
Leeman, Robert 87
Levy, Barnett 5

Lonely Soldiers' Guild 31, 34
Long, Chris 103
Lord Linlithgow, Governor-General 15
Luhrs (Luhers), Archibald 55
Luhrmann, Baz 93
Lyons, Samuel 4
Maclehose, James 4
Macrows Pty Ltd. 36
Mahony, Charles and Ann 3
Malvern Tramways Harmonica Band 69, 102
Manilla String Band 37
Marsh, Christian 105
Martin, Hedley 35
Martyn, Eleanor, 94
May, Clement 42
May, Florence 42
Mayger, James 53
McKinnon, Andrew 105
McMann, Stag 88
Meisel, C.W. 3
Melbourne Boys Club Mouth Organ Band 57, 68
Melbourne Ladies Crackajack Mouth Organ Band 50, 70
Melbourne Try Society 67
Messerschmidt, Dezider 65
Messner, Christian 3
Mick Simmons Pty Ltd 46, 64
Minson, Lawrie 93
Missin, Pat 42
Mitchell, T.J. 42, 53
Moore, Maggie 6, 7, 8, 93
Moore, Vern 82
Morley, Arthur 39
Morton, Tex 75, 76
Mouth Organ Band 42, 53
Mouth Organ Club 4BC, 4KQ 91
National Film & Sound Archive 103
Nicholson's Pty Ltd 96
Noonan, Chris 93
North Sydney Tramway Mouth Organ Band 98
Omond, Albert 20
Omond, Walter 20, 39, 42
Our Boys Institute 22
Paling W.H. & Co. 61
P.H. Brunnbauer 14
Polack, Abraham 2, 3
Queensland Football Club Band 17
Rainey, George 55
Ramage, Roy 69
Reid, Sir George 27
Reinlein, Georg Anton 3

Rhythmic Three 38
Richter, Joseph 3
Roberts, H.H. (Harry) 7
Robertson, Dick 97
Robinson, W.V. 58
Rockhampton Mouth Organ Band 71
Rhythm Reedz 85
Royal Agricultural Society NSW 16
Sadler, Harry 39
Sampson Mouth Organ Course 101
Schofield, Sam 35
Schreiner, Herb 88
Sculthorpe, Peter 93
Sebastian, John 88
Seydel & Son 17
Shalders, H.R. 'Dick' 97
Sick and Wounded Soldiers' Fund 34
Sinclair, James 57
Skurray, Bruce 86, 106
Smith, Laurie 86, 91
Smith, Rex 91
Smith, Sydney 3
Smits, Tricia and Jac 105
Smits Muzic 105
Smyth, Robert I. 61
Solomon, Braham 51
Spouse, P.C. 46, 50, 53, 98
Stevens, George 63
Sykes, A.P. 30
Tahiwis, 38
Tahiwi, Kingi 38
Tahiwi, Henare 38
"Taisei Maru" Harmonica Band 92
Tait, Charles 20, 21
Taylor, Superintendent 10
Theatre Royal Orchestra 5
Thomas & Co. 95
Thompson, Harry 75, 76, 77, 93, 98
Thompson, Jack 92, 93
Thompson, Peter 86
Thursday Island String Band 37
Trapp, H. 14
Trimmel and Zettl 12
Thie, Otto 14
Thie, Wilhelm 4, 14
Thie, Wilhelm Jnr. 14
Three Winds Trio 85
Twenty-First Regiment Band 5
Van Allen, Will 21, 39, 101
Victorian Mouth Organ Band 71

Victorian Mouth Organ Bands Association (VMOBA) 50, 51, 69, 70, 71
Victorian Patriotic Crackajack Band 34
Wallace, Doug 71
Walters, Brandon 93
Weiss Harmonica Factory 14, 58
W.H. Glen Pty Ltd 63
Wilhelm Thie 11, 12, 13, 14
Williamson, J.C. 6, 7, 8
Williamson, James 7
Williamson, John 10
Wilson, Mr 10
Woolworths Ltd 79, 89

www.ingramcontent.com/pod-product-compliance
Lightning Source LLC
Chambersburg PA
CBHW081924170426
43200CB00014B/2828